The Rockwool Foundation Research Unit

Study Paper No. 100

Job Creation and Job Types – New Evidence from Danish Entrepreneurs

Johan M. Kuhn, Nikolaj Malchow-Møller and Anders Sørensen

University Press of Southern Denmark

Odense 2015

Job Creation and Job Types – New Evidence from Danish Entrepreneurs

Study Paper No. 100

Published by:
The Rockwool Foundation research Unit and
University press of Southern Denmark

Address:
The Rockwool Foundation Research Unit
Soelvgade 10, 2.tv.
DK-1307 Copenhagen K

Telephone   +45 33 34 48 00
E-mail   forskningsenheden@rff.dk
web site: www.en.rff.dk

ISBN 978-87-93119-27-7
ISSN 0908-3979

November 2015

Job Creation and Job Types – New Evidence from Danish Entrepreneurs

Johan M. Kuhn, Department of International Economics and Management, Copenhagen Business School, Porcelænshaven 16A, DK-2000 Frederiksberg, Denmark (tel: +45 3815 3467, email: jmk.int@cbs.dk)

Nikolaj Malchow-Møller, Department of Business and Economics, University of Southern Denmark, Campusvej 55, 5230 Odense M, Denmark (tel: +45 6550 2109, email: nmm@sam.sdu.dk

Anders Sørensen (corresponding author), Department of Economics, Copenhagen Business School, Porcelænshaven 16A, DK-2000 Frederiksberg, Denmark (tel: +45 3815 3493, email: as.eco@cbs.dk).

Abstract:

We extend earlier analyses of the job creation of start-ups vs. established firms by taking into consideration the educational content of the jobs created and destroyed. We define education-specific measures of job creation and job destruction at the firm level, and we use these to construct a measure of "surplus job creation" defined as jobs created on top of any simultaneous destruction of similar jobs in incumbent firms in the same region and industry. Using Danish employer-employee data from 2002-7, which identify the start-ups and which cover almost the entire private sector, these measures allow us to provide a more nuanced assessment of the role of entrepreneurial firms in the job-creation process than previous studies. Our findings show that while start-ups are responsible for the entire overall net job creation, incumbents account for more than a third of net job creation within high-skilled jobs. Moreover, start-ups "only" create around half of the surplus jobs, and even less of the high-skilled surplus jobs. Finally, our approach allows us to characterize and identify differences across industries, educational groups and regions.

Keywords: Job creation, entrepreneurial firms, start-ups, surplus job creation
JEL: L26, J21, J31

Acknowledgements: We are grateful to the Rockwool Foundation for funding of this project, and Statistics Denmark for providing the data. We thank two referees, a guest editor, John Haltiwanger, Jan Rose Skaksen, Søren Leth-Petersen, Mette Ejrnæs, and participants at the Workshop on Economics of Entrepreneurship, June 29, 2015, Washington DC, for useful comments.

1 Introduction

The purpose of this paper is to develop a framework for comparing the job creation and job destruction by start-ups and established firms – a framework that distinguishes between different firm types and between different job types, and which takes the potential simultaneity in the creation and destruction of jobs across firms into account.

Entrepreneurs are generally considered as being of key importance for generating new jobs and economic growth in an increasingly competitive international environment. Such thoughts have given rise to initiatives such as the *Small Business Act for Europe* and the *SBIR* program in the USA; programmes that reallocate substantial resources from large established firms to small firms and start-ups.

The empirical testing of these issues on actual job data started back in the 1980's, when Birch (1981, 1987) claimed that small firms (many of which are young as well) are the main driver of US job creation. Birch (1987) found that firms with fewer than 20 employees accounted for 88% of overall employment growth in the USA between 1981 and 1985. In the wake of Birch's initial analyses, a large number of studies have analysed the role of small and new firms in the job-creation process using data on firm- or establishment-level worker flows. Most of these studies rely on the methodology developed in Davis and Haltiwanger (1992) and Davis *et al.* (1996a), who define measures of job creation and job destruction at the establishment level, which in turn can be used to construct measures of gross and net job creation (and destruction) at more aggregate levels, such as a firm, an industry or a size/age class of firms.

The majority of studies in the literature have focused on the job creation of small firms (or establishments) vs. large firms (or establishments); see, *e.g.*, Baldwin and Picot (1995), Wagner (1995), Davis *et al.* (1996a, b), Broersma and Gautier (1997), Hohti (2000), Barnes and Haskel (2002), and Neumark *et al.* (2011). The general message to emerge from this literature is that small firms (or establishments) tend to contribute more to both gross and net job creation than larger firms (or establishments).

Although start-ups are typically small, and small firms are often young, the two sets of firms are not identical, but the number of studies that have looked at the role of new establishments or new firms in the job-creation process is more limited. Examples include Dunne *et al.* (1989), Davis *et al.* (1996a), Klette and Mathiassen (1996), Spletzer (2000), Neumark *et al.* (2006), Malchow-Møller *et al.* (2011) and Haltiwanger *et al.* (2013). Among these, only Neumark *et al.* (2006), Malchow-Møller *et al.* (2011) and Haltiwanger *et al.* (2013) distinguish new establishments belonging to new firms from new establishments belonging to old firms. Still, the message that emerges from this literature is that new establishments or new firms contribute significantly more to gross and net job creation then older establishments/firms. In the most recent paper, Haltiwanger *et al.* (2013) actually find that once you control for firm age, there is no connection between firm size and net job creation. New firms can account for the entire net job creation in the economy.

However, most of the above-mentioned studies do not distinguish between different types of jobs, and those that do so are disaggregating by employer characteristics like industry; see, *e.g.*, Davis and Haltiwanger (1992) and Spletzer (2000). None of these studies distinguish between different types of jobs created (and destroyed) within a firm, probably due to a lack of data.[1] This necessarily limits what can be learned regarding the flows of different types of jobs. A positive job-creation figure for a given firm may thus hide substantial reallocations between different types of jobs within the firm. It could, *e.g.*, reflect that less-educated blue-collar workers have been laid off while highly-educated white-collar workers have been hired. Without data on the types of jobs involved, the different overall job-creation patterns of entrepreneurial firms and non-entrepreneurial firms documented in the literature may mask important underlying differences in the types of jobs created and destroyed. This is unfortunate if we are interested in, not only the number, but also the type and quality of jobs created by entrepreneurial and non-entrepreneurial firms.

Furthermore, job creation in one firm is likely to come to some extent at the expense of job destruction in other firms. Specifically, if the creation of jobs in one firm takes place within the same narrowly defined market, industry and/or area in which similar jobs are lost in other firms, then the "newness" of the jobs is likely to be lower than if jobs are created in industries, markets or areas where similar jobs are not lost. In the former case, the jobs

---

[1] The only paper that we have been able to find, which distinguishes between different types of jobs at the firm level, is a paper by Dunne *et al.* (1997), which studies the connections between changes in technology and the structure of wages and employment. In this paper, measures of job creation and job destruction for production and non-production workers, respectively, are constructed.

created may reflect simple displacements or reallocations of existing jobs, while the jobs created in the latter case are new to the local market. This distinction between jobs that potentially reflect displacement/reallocation of existing jobs and jobs that are new to the local job market is not captured by the existing gross- and net-job-creation measures, but might be extremely relevant for policy interventions aimed at job creation.[2]

In this paper, we address these two issues. We focus on job creation in start-ups vs. established firms, but as opposed to previous studies, we introduce a measure of education-specific job creation at the firm level. We base our analysis on Danish employer-employee register data for the time period 2002-2007 from *Statistics Denmark*. These data cover almost the entire private sector of the Danish economy, and they identify all organic start-ups (nascent firms) in a given year and thereby avoid misclassifications of organizational spin-offs of established firms as start-ups. Furthermore, the data contains detailed information about the educational background of all employees, which can be used to characterise the educational content of a job.

Applying these data sources allows us to distinguish between different types of jobs in our analysis of job creation. The disaggregation of jobs into types also enables us to link the creation of specific types of jobs in some firms directly to the destruction of the same types of jobs in other firms. Hence, we are able to construct a measure of "surplus job creation" defined as jobs created on top of any simultaneous destruction of similar jobs in established firms in the same region and industry. This in turn allows for a more nuanced assessment of the contribution of both entrepreneurial firms and established firms to job creation than if you only rely on the traditional measures of gross and net job creation. Gross job creation ignores any simultaneity between job creation and destruction across firms, while net job creation nets out everything and thereby ignores any differences across firms. Our measure of "surplus job creation", on the other hand, is an attempt to capture the extra jobs added to a local "job cluster" or "labour market", and to distinguish these from jobs created in a local job cluster/labour market where similar jobs are destroyed.

---

[2] While the issues of potential displacement/reallocation of jobs have not been the focus of the above-mentioned literature, they have been discussed in related strands of literature. Notably, analyses of employment growth at regional levels (*e.g.*, Audretsch and Fritsch, 2002; Fölster, 2000; and Fritsch and Müller, 2008) and analyses from the industrial organization realm (*e.g.*, Audretsch, 1995) are highly aware of job creation of start-ups potentially displacing jobs in established firms.

Although the main contribution of this paper is to develop an accounting framework for measuring job creation and job destruction by different types of firms, applying this framework to the Danish data leads to a number of derived contributions.

First, we demonstrate that our measure of "surplus job creation" in the Danish economy significantly exceeds the traditional measure of net job creation from Davis *et al.* (1996), but is substantially below the traditional measure of gross job creation also from Davis *et al.* (1996). Thus, our measure provides a different and complementary picture of the job-market dynamics.

Second, we show that a substantial share of the job creation in new firms is associated with a destruction of highly similar jobs in established firms. This might reflect that start-ups generate jobs that were previously destroyed by established firms, or, alternatively, that start-ups cause job destruction in established firms. The descriptive nature of the present analysis does not allow us to answer that question. However, it still shows that the new firms' contribution to aggregate employment growth may be far less than suggested by their net-job-creation numbers.

Third, our analysis qualifies previous estimates of the relative importance of established firms for job creation. We find that although overall net job creation in the period considered was negative in established firms, they still created between 35% and 60% of the "surplus" jobs. This indicates that not just start-ups, but also established firms are important for job creation.

Finally, we document a large heterogeneity in the relative importance of start-ups for job creation (both net and surplus job creation) across industries and education groups. Furthermore, the "newness" of the average job created by start-ups and established firms, respectively, also varies across industries, regions and education groups. Our framework allows us to identify industries or education groups where start-ups play a larger role for job creation, or where the job creation by start-ups is characterised by a larger share of surplus jobs. In particular, we find that established firms are more important for the generation of new high-skilled than new low-skilled jobs, and that the "newness" of high-skilled jobs in general is higher. Similarly, we find that entrepreneurial firms are more important for job creation within construction than manufacturing.

This might be highly relevant from a policy perspective. Our analysis is thus closely related to an on-going discussion in the literature about the factors or the "technological regimes" that make some industries, regions, *etc.* more favourable to start-ups, and others more favourable to established firms. The idea of different "regimes" were introduced by Nelson and Winter (1982) and Winter (1984) and has been refined and analysed in a number of studies including Audretsch (1995), Gort and Klepper (1982), Dosi (1982, 1988), Acs and Audretsch (1990), Malerba (1992), Malerba and Orsenico (1993), Agarwal (1998) and Audretsch and Fritsch (2002).

Shane (2009) has previously argued that policymakers ought to discriminate policy support between different kinds of start-ups, but there is little guidance in the literature on how to do this. The extent to which start-ups are creating "surplus jobs" might be considered a relevant criterion, and support could then be targeted towards industries/groups where this is more likely to be the case.

To get a first impression of whether surplus jobs, and especially those created in start-ups, are more productive and/or of a higher quality than other jobs, we conclude the paper with a decomposition analysis of the development in the average wage level. Using decomposition techniques suggested by Foster *et al.* (2001) and Griliches and Regev (1995), we find that the contribution to average wage growth from job clusters with surplus jobs corresponds roughly to their share in employment, and that new jobs generated by start-ups seem to be of "average quality" as they do not contribute to the growth in average wages.

The rest of the paper is organised as follows: Section 2 describes our data, while Section 3 outlines the empirical approach. Results are presented in Section 4, and Section 5 contains a number of robustness analyses. Section 6 performs a decomposition exercise, while Section 7 concludes. An appendix with additional tables is added at the end.

2 Data

We use matched worker-firm data covering almost the entire private sector of the Danish economy for the period 2002-7. The data are drawn from different Danish registers administered by *Statistics Denmark*.

First, the *General Enterprise Statistics* builds on the *Central Business Register* and contains annual information about all active firms in the Danish economy. From this database, we get the firm identifier, the industry and the region of all firms in the private sector.

Second, the *Statistics on New Enterprises* identifies all firm start-ups in a given year. This database is thus a subsample of the *General Enterprise Statistics* and includes firms that fulfil a number of conditions that allow us to consider them as being newly started (nascent) firms in a given year, *i.e.*, organic start-ups. There are between approximately 17,000 (2002) and 24,000 (2007) firm start-ups per year in the database.

Note that Statistics Denmark has undertaken extensive efforts to identify the organic start-ups. Many of the formally new firms may thus be the result of restructurings or the result of organizing existing or additional activities in formally new enterprises. As a consequence, a firm that appears in the *Statistics on New Enterprises* must not only be newly registered for VAT at the business authorities, it is also required that the firm has not existed previously under a different name/company, with a different owner, or in another legal form (sole proprietorship, partnership, corporation, etc.). Furthermore, sole proprietorships held by an individual who has already registered for taxable activities are excluded.[3] Finally, the data are cleaned for registrations that are due to re-starts of businesses after closure or changes in the firm-registration information. Thus, the set of start-ups used in this paper is more likely to reflect the organic entrepreneurial start-ups than if we had just used all new establishments or all new firms, as has been common practice in the literature.

The *Statistics on New Enterprises* is restricted to industries that *Statistics Denmark* categorises as "private urban functions". This excludes the public sector and (most of) the primary sector, as well as industries with activities that are not liable to VAT, such as

---

[3] We do not know how many new firms were eliminated as a result of this latter restriction, but if some entrepreneurs start multiple sole proprietorships, there is a risk that this restriction may eliminate some observations from the data that might be considered as organic start-ups. On the other hand, it seems reasonable to assume (and require) that entrepreneurs that start multiple ventures, and where the ventures should also be considered as separate firms, will (and must) choose another legal form than sole proprietorship (*e.g.*, a corporation) for the different ventures. At least from a financial perspective, different sole proprietorships held by the same individual will not be independent entities.

dentists, transportation of persons, banking *etc.*[4] Furthermore, the *Statistics on New Enterprises* is restricted to standard ownership types.[5] To ensure valid comparisons, we impose the same sampling conditions on the *General Enterprise Statistics*, *i.e.* we exclude firms in that are not in private urban functions and firms with non-standard ownership types. This leaves us with 160,000 firms in 2002 and 192,000 firms in 2007.

Third, the *Firm Integrated Database (FIDA)* identifies all the individuals working in a given firm in the last week of November each year. This allows us to construct the number of jobs in any given firm in any given year as the simple headcount of the number of employees (including the owner in sole proprietorships and partnerships) in the last week of November. Note that we only consider firms with at least one individual present, *i.e.*, we exclude incorporated firms without employees.

In the analysis below, we look at job creation over a five-year time period from 2002 to 2007, as 2007 is the last year before a data-break in the *FIDA*. In this way we also avoid any influence from the Great Recession. The start-ups in our analysis are those firms that are identified as having been established after 2002 according to the *Statistics on New Enterprises,* whereas the established firms are those that existed already in the initial year, 2002.

We follow *Statistics Denmark* and allow for up to two jobs per individual per year at the census date in November. That is, we allow for a primary occupation and a secondary occupation. This results in 1.80 million different jobs (firm-worker relationships) in 2002, held by 1.69 million different individuals. As the data are from a period with relatively strong

---

[4] These industries are not included as the basis for the *Statistics on New Enterprises* are firms that register for VAT. Hence, we do not have information about new firms that are not liable to VAT. Private sector service firms that are excluded from the analysis are firms within service sectors: child day-care activities, primary education, general secondary education, higher education, nursing homes, activities of household employers, other service activities, general medical practice activities including dentists, hospital activities, real estate agencies etc., and mortgage credit institutes. In total, only 0.44 percent of all firms in the private sector (excluding the primary sector) are found in the sub-sectors not liable to VAT.

[5] Non-standard ownership types are rare but include administration of estates, foundations, associations, municipalities, regions, and church councils. Around 2.7 percent of all firms in the private sector (excluding the primary sector) are excluded because they have non-standard ownership types.

economic growth, the number of jobs increases to 1.95 million in 2007, held by 1.83 million different individuals.

Note that we are not discriminating between "good" and "bad" jobs based on thresholds for income or hours worked, or whether or not the job is a given person's main occupation. Implementing such additional conditions would probably reduce the number of jobs in start-ups, as, *e.g.*, more jobs in start-ups are held by individuals who are having this job as their secondary occupation, and since previous research like Malchow-Møller *et al.* (2011) and Wagner (1994) suggest that a larger share of jobs in start-ups would fall short of minimum income thresholds.

Finally, the *FIDA* also allows us to retrieve information about the individuals' educational background from *Statistics Denmark*'s education registers. These registers contain data on the educational attainment of the individual, which in turn is used to characterise the educational (skill) content of a job.[6] In the main analysis, we distinguish between six different education groups where information is defined by the length and type of the education programme (and following the Danish Education Classification system): Primary schooling (up to 9 years); vocational training (12 years); high school (12 years), short further education (13-14 years); medium further education (15-16 years); long further education (17+ years). We also apply a seventh (residual) group for individuals with missing information about educational attainment.

3 Methodology

In this section, we describe the empirical approach used in the paper. We start in Section 3.1 by defining job creation and job destruction at the firm level taking the educational content of a job into account. In Section 3.2, we introduce our new measure of "surplus job creation". Section 3.3 then splits up the different measures into contributions from start-up

---

[6] An alternative approach would be to classify the jobs according to the tasks and duties undertaken in the jobs using, *e.g.*, ISCO codes. Unfortunately, such data are only available for few jobs and the data quality is low as it is self-reported by the employers. One drawback of using the educational attainment of individuals as our measure of skill content is that some jobs where only limited skills are required might in practice be filled by individuals with, *e.g.*, a higher education. This potentially introduces some noise into the analysis stemming from people being underemployed. However, we do not expect this to constitute a major problem in the Danish economy.

(entrepreneurial) firms and incumbent (established) firms, while Section 3.4 shows how the firm-specific measures can be aggregated to different levels of interest, *e.g.*, the industry level. We also define a number of key indicators of job creation to be used in the subsequent empirical analysis. Finally, in Section 3.5, we discuss the choice of an appropriate size of the education-industry-region clusters when measuring surplus job creation.

3.1 Job creation and job destruction at the firm level

Job creation and job destruction at the firm level are typically measured using the method developed by Davis and Haltiwanger (1992) and Davis *et al.* (1996a). Following their approach, gross job creation, C_{it}, and gross job destruction, D_{it}, at firm *i* between year $t-5$ and *t* are defined as:

$$C_{it} = \max(X_{it} - X_{it-5}, 0)$$
$$D_{it} = \max(X_{it-5} - X_{it}, 0)$$

where X_{it} is employment of firm *i* in year *t*.[7] The variable C_{it} is thus equal to the increase in the number of employees if an increase has occurred. If the number of employees has decreased, the variable equals zero. Similarly, D_{it} equals the number of jobs lost if employment has decreased, and it equals zero if employment has increased. Note that start-ups have $X_{it-5} = 0$ by construction, while exiting firms have $X_{it} = 0$. Aggregate job creation and aggregate job destruction are then found by summing C_{it} and D_{it}, respectively, across firms, and net job creation at the aggregate level is found as the difference between these.

These standard measures of job creation and job destruction at the firm level ignore any differences in job characteristics. Thus, job creation in firm *i* is the same whether it opens up two blue-collar jobs in production or it opens up 10 white-collar jobs in R&D while at the same time closing down eight blue-collar jobs in production. In both cases, two jobs have been created, and hence $C_{it} = 2$ and $D_{it} = 0$.

---

[7] Note that in this paper we measure job creation and destruction over a five-year time interval. This is different from most studies of job creation, which are typically based on annual employment changes. The choice to consider job creation over an extended time interval is motivated by our focus on job creation by entrepreneurial firms where jobs might take some years to materialise. Also we want to avoid picking up temporary year-to-year fluctuations. We consider job creation over a three-year time interval as a robustness check in Section 5.

However, in the latter case, 10 high-skilled jobs were created while eight low-skill jobs were destroyed, and the consequences of this are likely to be very different from the creation of two additional high-skilled jobs. It is unlikely that any of the eight workers laid off in production will occupy any of the 10 R&D jobs created. The traditional measures of job creation and destruction at the firm level are silent on the types of jobs created by a firm, but if we are to understand the labour-market consequences, we should distinguish between jobs with different requirements. One way to do this is to distinguish between jobs with different skill (educational) content.

Specifically, we can define firm i's education-specific job creation and destruction, i.e., creation and destruction of jobs of education type e, as follows:

$$C_{it}^e = \max(X_{it}^e - X_{it-5}^e, 0)$$

$$D_{it}^e = \max(X_{it-5}^e - X_{it}^e, 0)$$

where X_{it}^e is the employment of workers with education type e in firm i in year t (in what follows, we drop the time subscript to simplify notation). Thus, if we distinguish between seven education groups, as we do in the main part of the analysis below, we have seven measures of job creation/destruction at the firm level. These measures can be aggregated across education groups within a given firm to arrive at our alternative firm-level measures of gross job creation and destruction, GJC_i and GJD_i:

$$GJC_i = \sum_e C_i^e \geq C_i$$

$$GJD_i = \sum_e D_i^e \geq D_i.$$

Note that the distinction between jobs with different skill content (weakly) increases the total gross job creation and destruction for any given firm, compared to the traditional measures, C_i and D_i. The reason is that the firm can now have job creation in one education group and job destruction in another education group. In the example used above, firm i would have $GJC_i = 10$ and $GJD_i = 8$. However, net job creation at the firm level is still the same as before, $NJC_i = GJC_i - GJD_i = C_i - D_i = 2$, independently of how many skill groups we distinguish between.[8]

---

[8] We measure job creation and destruction at the firm level, whereas Davis and Haltiwanger (1992) and Davis et al. (1996a) measure job creation and destruction at the establishment level. This introduces a potential measurement error in relation to mergers and acquisitions. Specifically, if a firm buys an old firm or an old

3.2 Surplus job creation

Distinguishing between jobs with different skill content gives us a more nuanced picture of the actual job creation and destruction within a given firm. Still, much of the job creation we observe within individual firms could reflect reallocations of existing jobs. As an example, if a neighbouring firm j closes down six white-collar jobs at the same time as firm i opens up 10 white-collar jobs, then some of these 10 jobs may reflect displacements or reallocations of the jobs in firm j. Thus, if we think of the white-collar jobs in these neighbouring firms, as some sort of "local labour market", only four white-collar jobs have been added (are in surplus) at this market.

In order to try and distinguish potential displacements and reallocations of jobs from the creation of such "surplus" jobs, we introduce the idea of a "job cluster" that we like to think of as an approximation to a local labour market. We define job clusters by the skill content of the job, the industry of the firm, and the regional location of the firm, but alternative or additional dimensions could be the job function or the product market of the firm (if that information was available). A job cluster, (e, c), thus consists of all jobs of a certain education type, e, within a given industry-region cell, c. *I.e.*, a cluster should ideally contain similar types of jobs, where it is relatively easy for an individual to switch between jobs, whereas it is more difficult to switch to jobs in other clusters. In that case, we can think of the clusters as local labour markets.

The gross job creation and gross job destruction within a job cluster, GJC_c^e and GJD_c^e, are found by aggregating the education-specific job creation and destruction measures, respectively, across all firms within that job cluster:

---

establishment from another firm, this will be included in the acquiring firm's measure of job creation. In this way, mergers and acquisitions can work to overstate the amount of actual job creation (and destruction) from an establishment-level perspective. On the other hand, if we define job creation at the establishment level, then reallocations among plants within a firm will influence the amount of total job creation, which is also unfortunate. Hence, there is a trade-off here. However, we do not consider this to be of quantitative importance as the vast majority of Danish firms are one-establishment firms.

$$GJC_c^e = \sum_{i \in c} C_i^e$$

$$GJD_c^e = \sum_{i \in c} D_i^e.$$

The net job creation in a cluster is then given by the difference between the two measures above:

$$NJC_c^e = GJC_c^e - GDC_c^e = \sum_{i \in c}(C_i^e - D_i^e).$$

"Surplus job creation", *SJC*, is defined as the jobs created on top of any simultaneous destruction of similar jobs in similar firms within the same region. In other words, in job clusters with positive net job creation, the number of surplus jobs is given by the net job creation within that job cluster. Clusters with negative net job creation, on the other hand, generate no surplus jobs by definition:

$$SJC_c^e = \max(NJC_c^e, 0).$$

The amount of surplus job creation in a job cluster is, of course, sensitive to the cluster definition used. We return to this issue below.[9]

3.3 Start-Up Firms vs. Incumbent Firms

To measure the relative importance of start-up and incumbent firms with respect to job creation, we split the gross job creation, GJC_c^e, and the net job creation, NJC_c^e, within a job cluster into contributions from start-ups (*su*) and incumbents (*in*):

$$GJC_c^e = GJC_{in \in c}^e + GJC_{su \in c}^e = \sum_{i \in in \cap c} C_i^e + \sum_{i \in su \cap c} C_i^e$$

$$NJC_c^e = NJC_{in \in c}^e + NJC_{su \in c}^e = \sum_{i \in in \cap c}(C_i^e - D_i^e) + \sum_{i \in su \cap c} C_i^e$$

---

[9] Note also that a firm may have several establishments, and even though the establishments of a firm may be located in different regions, their job creation/destruction is included in the region where the firm (the headquarter) is located. By using the firm as the unit of observation we avoid counting reallocations within the firm, from, *e.g.*, an establishment in region 1 to an establishment in region 2, as surplus job creation. The flip side of this is that a firm may be located in region 1, but creates jobs in an establishment in region 2. These jobs are at the risk of being netted out against jobs destroyed by other firms or establishments in region 1 or even by an establishment in, say, region 3, but owned by a firm located in region 1.

where $GJC^e_{in\epsilon c}$ and $GJC^e_{su\epsilon c}$ are the gross creation of jobs by incumbent firms and start-up firms, respectively, within cluster (e, c), and similarly for the *NJC* measures. Note that net job creation for start-ups equals their gross job creation, $NJC^e_{su\epsilon c} = GJC^e_{su\epsilon c}$, as start-ups have no job destruction by definition. This also implies that the total gross job destruction within a job cluster is given by the gross job destruction by the incumbent firms, $GJC^e_c = GJC^e_{in\epsilon c}$.

The surplus job creation within a job cluster can also be split into contributions from incumbent firms and start-ups. For incumbent firms, the number of surplus jobs generated, $SJC^e_{in\epsilon c}$, is equal to their net job creation (if positive), as start-ups have no net destruction by definition. Thus, $SJC^e_{in\epsilon c} = \max(NJC^e_{in\epsilon c}, 0)$. For start-ups, the amount of surplus job creation, $SJC^e_{su\epsilon c}$, equals their net job creation less any net job destruction by incumbents in the same job cluster. If net job creation by start-ups is less than the net job destruction by incumbents, the number of surplus jobs created by start-ups is zero. Formally, this can be written as follows:

$$SJC^e_c = SJC^e_{in\epsilon c} + SJC^e_{su\epsilon c} = \max(NJC^e_{in\epsilon c}, 0) + \max(NJC^e_{su\epsilon c} - \max(-NJC^e_{in\epsilon c}, 0), 0).$$

3.4 Aggregate Measures and Key Indicators

The above measures can all be aggregated in various ways across job clusters to obtain, e.g., the net creation of jobs of education type e within a given industry, or the gross creation of all types of jobs in a given region. More formally, gross and net job creation for aggregate group A, where A is a collection of job clusters, are given by:

$$GJC_A = \sum_{(e,c) \in A} GJC^e_c = GJC^{in}_A + GJC^{su}_A = \sum_{(e,c) \in A} GJC^e_{in\epsilon c} + \sum_{(e,c) \in A} GJC^e_{su\epsilon c}$$

$$NJC_A = \sum_{(e,c) \in A} NJC^e_c = NJC^{in}_A + NJC^{su}_A = \sum_{(e,c) \in A} NJC^e_{in\epsilon c} + \sum_{(e,c) \in A} NJC^e_{su\epsilon c}$$

where GJC^{in}_A and GJC^{su}_A are the gross creation of jobs by incumbent firms and start-up firms, respectively, in A. These are found by summing over all the incumbent and start-up firms, respectively, in the clusters belonging to A.[10] Similarly, NJC_A^{in} and NJC_A^{su} are the net creation of jobs by incumbent firms and start-up firms, respectively, in A.

Finally, the amount of surplus job creation for aggregate group A is given by:

$$SJC_A = \sum_{(e,c) \in A} SJC_c^e = SJC_A^{in} + SJC_A^{su} = \sum_{(e,c) \in A} SJC_{in \in c}^e + \sum_{(e,c) \in A} SJC_{su \in c}^e$$

where SJC_A^{in} and SJC_A^{su} are the creation of surplus jobs by incumbent firms and start-up firms, respectively, in A.

These aggregate measures can in turn be used to define a number of key indicators that can be used to characterise the job creation and job destruction patterns of, *e.g.*, different industries, education groups or regions. First, to evaluate the importance of start-ups' job creation relative to the job creation by incumbents, we will consider the start-ups' share of job creation in group A:[11]

$$\text{Start} - \text{up's share of } GJC_A = \frac{GJC_A^{su}}{GJC_A}$$

$$\text{Start} - \text{up's share of } SJC_A = \frac{SJC_A^{su}}{SJC_A}$$

Second, to characterise the "newness" of the jobs created by start-up firms and incumbent firms, respectively, we will consider the amount of surplus job creation relative to the amount of gross job creation by incumbents and start-ups, respectively, in group A:[12]

$$\text{Newness of jobs created by incumbents in A} = \frac{SJC_A^{in}}{GJC_A^{in}}$$

$$\text{Newness of jobs created by start} - \text{ups in A} = \frac{SJC_A^{su}}{GJC_A^{su}}.$$

---

[10] Note that when NJC_A involves aggregating across all education groups within one or more industry-region cells, it becomes identical to the net-job-creation measure defined by Davis and Haltiwanger (1992) for the same industry-region cells.

[11] Note that the start-ups' share of net job creation is not always well defined, as aggregate net job creation may be negative.

[12] Note that since the net job creation by incumbent firms might be negative in some clusters, the ratio of surplus jobs to net job creation is more difficult to interpret and therefore omitted.

3.5 Definition of Job Clusters

The choice of cluster size will obviously matter for the resulting measure of surplus job creation. The purpose of introducing a job cluster is to distinguish between displacements/reallocations and the creation of surplus/additional jobs in a local labour market. Jobs within a cluster should therefore ideally be relatively similar and individuals should relatively easily be able to take up other jobs within a cluster, while taking up jobs in other clusters is more difficult. Only in that case is it reasonable to think of a job cluster as a local labour market and to net out job creation and destruction within a cluster, but not across clusters, when measuring surplus job creation.

If we use broad industries, regions and skill groups, there is a risk of netting out jobs that are actually very different and difficult to switch between, while if we use more narrowly defined industries, regions and skill groups, we might end up counting jobs as surplus jobs even though they reflect reallocations across, say, two neighbouring regions or industries. Thus, in the former case, we are likely to get a more conservative estimate of surplus job creation, while in the latter case, we get a more optimistic estimate.

As we want a cluster to reflect a local labour market, the regional dimension should ideally identify areas where an individual is able to fill a job vacancy without having to relocate. The natural choice here is to use the five administrative regions in Denmark. These have an average size of approximately 8,500 square kilometres and hence represent areas within which commuting is feasible at a reasonable cost. Similarly, the industry and educational classifications used should ideally identify industries and education groups within which common skills can be identified.

The strategy we use in the following is to use a baseline cluster definition for most of the analysis and then subsequently investigate the sensitivity of the obtained results with respect to the choice of cluster definition. In the baseline cluster definition, we distinguish between seven education groups (defined by the length and type of the education programmes), the five administrative regions and 233 industries, corresponding to the 3-digit NACE level. Potentially, this results in 8,155 job clusters. However, a number of these clusters are empty, leaving us with 7,175 clusters in total. In the empirical sections below, alternative cluster definitions are introduced to investigate the robustness of the results obtained with the baseline cluster definition. Specifically, all results are also presented in the appendix using 77 industries, corresponding to the 2-digit NACE level. This results in a total of 2,695 potential clusters of which 2,585 clusters are non-empty. Furthermore, the appendix also contains results where we omit the regional dimension in the cluster definition.

4 Results

In this section, we present the results of the empirical analysis. First, the results for aggregate gross and net job creation are described in Section 4.1, before we move on to the surplus jobs in Section 4.2. In both subsections, we analyse the importance of start-ups vs. incumbents and the robustness of the results with respect to the number of education groups, industries and regions used. In Section 4.3, we present results for different education groups, while Section 4.4 presents results at the industry level. Section 5 contains a number of robustness analyses, whereas Section 6 investigates the productivity or quality of jobs by decomposing the development in average wages.

4.1 Aggregate Gross and Net Job Creation

Table 1 presents the aggregate amounts of (education-specific) job creation and job destruction in the Danish economy, GJC_A, GJD_A and NJC_A, where A in this case is the (entire) private sector of the economy (excluding the primary sector). Note that these measures do not depend on the number of industries and regions used in the definition of job clusters, but only on the number of education groups used.

In the first row of the Table, we use just one education group. The measures then correspond to the original definitions of gross and net job creation from Davis and Haltiwanger (1992). In this case, GJC_A is simply the total increase in employment in those firms that grew between 2002 and 2007. Together these firms employed GJC_A = 814,594 extra workers in 2007 compared to 2002. Similarly, GJD_A is the total reduction in employment in those firms that contracted between 2002 and 2007. As can be seen, these firms destroyed 665,807 jobs, corresponding to 37% of the total employment in 2002. This bears evidence of a considerable reallocation of jobs across firms in the period considered. The net job creation between 2002 and 2007 was thus 148,787 jobs, which is an increase in employment of almost 10%. This reflects a boom in the Danish economy (and in most of the world) during this period. In Denmark, the unemployment rate fell below 3% in 2007.

The following columns break down the gross- and net-job-creation measures into contributions from incumbent firms, GJC_A^{in} and NJC_A^{in}, and start-ups, GJC_A^{su} and NJC_A^{su}, respectively. Remember that while job creation takes place in both types of firms, job destruction can only occur in incumbent firms by definition. Thus, for start-ups, the gross- and net-job-creation measures are always identical and positive; 218,059 jobs in this case. For incumbent firms, on the other hand, net job creation is typically negative as these firms are responsible for all the job destruction and only part of the job creation. In the present case, the net job creation of the incumbent firms was NJC_A^{in}= -69,272, which in turn reflects that growing incumbent firms increased their employment by 600,000 jobs, but also that the shrinking incumbent firms reduced their employment by 670,000 jobs. Thus, while the entire net job creation in the period considered can be accounted for by start-ups, only around 27% of the gross job creation took place in those firms.

The second row presents the results for our baseline case, where we use seven different education groups. In this case, GJC_A is the sum of the education-specific gross job creation across firms. This raises the overall amount of gross job creation by around 70,000 jobs compared to row 1 (and gross job destruction increases by a similar amount). These extra jobs reflect that some incumbent firms expanded their employment of, *e.g.*, high-skilled workers, while they reduced their employment of low-skilled workers. In row 1, only the firm-level change in employment is registered and added to either GJC_A or GJD_A, whereas in row 2 an increase in the number of high-skilled workers will add to GJC_A, while a reduction in low-skilled workers will add to GJD_A. The distinction between different education groups does therefore not affect the net-job-creation measure, nor does it affect the gross job creation by start-ups.

In row 3, we distinguish between 32 education groups (defined by length and subject). This further raises overall gross job creation to 915,316 jobs. This is approximately 12% more than in row 1. This overall increase reflects an increase of approximately 17% among incumbent firms from a gross creation of 596,535 jobs when using the traditional measure in row 1 to 697,257 jobs when using 32 education groups as in row 3. For start-ups, gross job creation equals 218,059 jobs in the period considered, independently of the number of education groups used. This implies that start-ups' share of gross job creation was between 23.8% and 26.8%, as shown in the last column of Table 1.

[Table 1 around here]

4.2 Surplus Job Creation

Based on the net-job-creation measure, we are tempted to conclude that incumbent firms did not create any new jobs in the period considered, while using the gross-job-creation measure, we get the impression that they created most of the jobs (75%). None of these measures are, however, fully informative about the actual creation of new jobs by incumbent firms and start-up firms, respectively. Some of the net job creation in start-ups may reflect closings of similar jobs in established firms, and just because net job creation is negative for incumbent firms on average, this does not mean that there was no creation of jobs in these firms; see also Haltiwanger *et al.* (2013) for a recent discussion of these issues.

Table 2 shows the aggregate amount of "surplus job creation" in the private sector using our new measure from Section 3. The Table also presents separate numbers for incumbent firms and start-up firms, respectively. For comparison, we also include the measures of gross and net job creation from Table 1. The first row contains the results when using our baseline job-cluster definition, while the following rows contain results for alternative cluster definitions. Thus, in rows 2-6, we vary the number of industries, while rows 7-9 and rows 10-12 vary the number of education groups and regions, respectively. In the two last rows, we use a single job cluster (row 13) and our most detailed cluster definition (row 14), respectively, where the latter results in a total of 80,221 different job clusters. Note that while aggregate net job creation is independent of the cluster definition, and aggregate gross job creation only depends on the number of education groups (and only for incumbent firms), the number of surplus jobs created by both incumbent and start-up firms depends on all three cluster dimensions.

[Table 2 around here]

Consider first the results for *all firms*. Using our baseline cluster definition with 7,175 different clusters, the first row in the Table shows that the total amount of surplus job creation in the economy equalled almost 290,000 jobs. In other words, 290,000 workers were added in those job clusters that grew in size between 2002 and 2007.[13] This should be compared with an overall net-job-creation measure of approximately 150,000 jobs. In other words, almost twice as many surplus jobs as net jobs were created, which shows that the traditional net-job-creation measure is likely to ignore important aspects of the job-creation process. The flip side of this difference between net job creation and surplus true job creation is that around 140,000 jobs were also genuinely destroyed in the period considered, *i.e.*, they were not replaced by similar jobs in other firms in the same industry and region.

The amount of surplus job creation decreases if we distinguish between fewer job clusters (as in rows 2-4, 7, 10 and 13), since this implies more netting out. If two distinct job clusters are merged, where one creates jobs while the other destructs jobs, it will reduce our measure of surplus job creation as only their total net job creation will now count towards the number of surplus jobs. If both clusters create jobs net, their net contribution is unaffected. For the same reason, increasing the number of job clusters raises the total amount of surplus job creation (see rows 6, 9, 12 and 14). As an example, distinguishing between just 77 industries (as in row 4) reduces the number of surplus jobs created to around 250,000, while distinguishing between 617 industries (row 6) increases the number to around 340,000. Similarly, if we do not distinguish between education groups, the number of surplus jobs is "just" around 260,000 (row 7), while it increases to around 305,000 if we distinguish between 32 education groups (row 9). In the extreme case where we only use one job cluster (row 13), surplus job creation simply equals net job creation. In sum, depending on the number of job clusters used, the number of surplus jobs created varies between 150,000 (one cluster) and 408,000 (80,221 clusters).

The following columns of the Table illustrate the contributions from incumbent firms and start-up firms, respectively. Using our baseline cluster definition, incumbent firms created almost 150,000 surplus jobs. If we increase (decrease) the number of job clusters, surplus job creation by incumbent firms rises (falls) for the same reasons as above. The more job clusters that are distinguished, the less likely it is that job creation by established firm i is offset by any job destruction by a "similar" firm j. Conversely, in the case with just one job cluster, surplus job creation by established firms cannot exceed their net job creation.

---

[13] Note that most of the surplus jobs were created in clusters that already existed in 2002. Thus, for the baseline cluster definition, only around 0.3% of all surplus jobs were created in clusters that did not exist in 2002.

While start-ups created almost the same amount of surplus jobs (140,000) as incumbent firms when using our baseline job-cluster definition, the effect of a more detailed cluster definition is less clear in their case. A larger number of job clusters may thus imply both more or less netting out. If the creation of jobs in start-ups takes place at the expense of jobs lost in incumbent firms within the same narrowly defined cluster, then distinguishing between fewer clusters may actually increase the number of surplus jobs created by start-ups, as it may increase internal netting out among established firms in previously different clusters. As an example, consider a situation with two job clusters where net job creation among incumbent firms is 10 in the first and –10 in the second, while net job creation by start-ups is zero in the first and 10 in the second cluster. Distinguishing between the two clusters result in a total of 10 surplus jobs by incumbents, and 0 by start-ups, while adding the clusters together, reduces the amount of surplus job creation by incumbents to zero, while it raises the amount of surplus job creation by start-ups to 10. Thus, in the extreme case with just one cluster (row 13), the amount of surplus job creation by start-ups is, in fact, slighter higher than when using the baseline cluster definition with 7,175 clusters (row 1).

Overall, it appears that the amount of surplus job creation by start-ups is not affected much when we change the cluster definition, while surplus job creation by incumbents increases with the number of job clusters used. As a consequence, the contribution of start-up firms to the total amount of surplus job creation becomes smaller (larger) if we increase (decrease) the number of clusters, as shown in the third last column of Table 2. For the one-cluster case (row 13), their share equals 100%, but for cluster choices that are not too far from the baseline cluster definition, start-ups' share is in the range of 40% to 65%, decreasing to 34% if we distinguish between 80,221 clusters (row 14).

Thus, even when accounting for the fact that some of the net job creation by start-ups is at the expense of similar jobs in established firms, start-ups still account for a significant share (roughly 50%) of the surplus job creation. However, the results also show that the contribution of established firms to the creation of surplus new jobs is substantial (50% or more) as soon as job types are assumed to be as specific as in our baseline scenario. This is the case even though the net job creation of incumbent firms has been clearly negative in the period considered and hence may give the impression that established firms did not contribute. Hopefully, this clearly illustrates how the SJC measure helps providing a more nuanced picture of the actual contribution of established firms to the job creation in the economy than the traditional gross- and net-job-creation measures can do by themselves.

Both start-ups and incumbent firms thus play an important role for the generation of surplus jobs, but what is the share of the gross jobs created by these firms that are surplus jobs, *i.e.*, in excess of cluster-specific job destruction in incumbent firms? The last two columns in Table 2 show that when using our baseline cluster definition, start-ups created 0.64 surplus jobs for each gross job they created. For established firms, only 22% of all gross jobs created were surplus jobs. Put differently, for each education-specific job created by a start-up, 0.36 jobs at the same educational level were destroyed by established firms in the same region and industry. For each job created by established firms, 0.78 jobs were destroyed in other established firms in the same job cluster. In other words, gross job creation of established firms is to a far greater extent characterized by "reshuffling" of individuals within the same cluster than is the case for start-ups.

Note further that our measure of the newness of the jobs created by start-ups is relatively robust towards changes in the job-cluster definition. For cluster choices that are reasonably close to the baseline definition, the measure is in the range of 62% to 68%. The corresponding measure for established firms, on the other hand, is more sensitive to changes in the cluster definition. For cluster choices in the neighbourhood of our baseline definition, the share of surplus jobs in gross job creation is in the range of 11% to 31%.

To sum up, using our baseline cluster definition, the amount of surplus job creation is almost twice as high as the amount of net job creation, and it reveals that both start-ups and established firms are heavily involved in adding jobs to local labour markets. However, while start-ups and established firms contribute almost equally to the total number of surplus jobs, the "newness" of the average job created is much more pronounced among start-ups.

4.3 Education-Level Results

In Table 3, we exploit our education-specific measures of job creation to consider the aggregate job creation for different education groups. The Table presents the results for seven different education groups using our baseline cluster definition. Consider first the results for *all firms* (columns 2-4). Here, gross job creation equalled 261,355 jobs for *primary schooling*. In other words, more than 260,000 additional unskilled jobs (*i.e.*, jobs filled by persons with only primary schooling) were added in those firms that increased their employment of unskilled workers between 2002 and 2007. This corresponds to 48% of the unskilled jobs in 2002. However, an almost similar amount of unskilled jobs were destroyed in firms that reduced their employment of workers with only primary schooling. Hence, net creation of unskilled jobs was less than 23,000 in the period considered. Still, among the 261,355 gross unskilled jobs created, more than 75,000 were not counteracted by reductions in unskilled jobs in other firms within the same industry-region cell. In other words, the growing unskilled job clusters created 75,000 surplus jobs ($SJC_A = 75,175$), while the shrinking unskilled job clusters destroyed 52,000 jobs.

In absolute terms, gross job creation was highest for the low-skilled groups (*primary schooling* and *vocational education*), but in relative terms it was around 50% of the initial employment for all education groups (slightly higher for *long further education*). Net job creation, on the other hand – although positive for all education groups – is considerably higher in relative terms for the three groups of *further education*. Thus, net job creation relative to employment in 2002 equalled 33% for jobs requiring a *long further education* and only 4% for jobs requiring only *primary schooling*.[14] This is not very surprising given the development in the educational attainment of the labour force in general. The differences across groups when it comes to surplus job creation are similar, but smaller. Thus, the number of surplus jobs relative to initial employment equalled 37% for jobs requiring a *long further education* and only 14% for jobs with *primary schooling*.

It is worth noticing that it is especially among the low-skilled groups that we observe a big difference between net job creation and the number of surplus jobs. The groups of *primary schooling* and *vocational education* are responsible for more than half of the surplus job creation but only around 25% of the net job creation. In other words, the net-job-creation measure hides the fact that many surplus low-skilled jobs were indeed created. This is because other low-skilled jobs were genuinely destroyed in other industry-region cells at the same time. For the group of *long further education*, the picture is different. Here net job

---

[14] Strictly speaking, we do not know whether the jobs *require* a long further education, we can only see that the jobs are filled by persons with a long further education. Thus, we are measuring jobs occupied by individuals with different educational backgrounds.

creation is only slightly lower than the number of surplus jobs, which shows that relatively few high-skilled jobs were genuinely destroyed between 2002 and 2007.

The next columns consider the contributions of incumbent firms and start-up firms separately. Note that start-ups were responsible for 25% of the gross job creation, and that this share is relatively constant across education groups. This is not the case, when we consider net job creation. Here, incumbent firms had negative contributions for the low-skilled groups (*primary schooling*, *vocational education*, and *high school*). Still, they created close to half of the surplus jobs in these groups – and the contribution of incumbent firms to surplus job creation in the groups of further education is even higher. In other words, start-ups are most important for the creation of surplus low-skilled jobs. For the group of *long further education*, it was established firms that created the lion's share (almost 2/3) of the surplus jobs.

Among the jobs created by start-ups and incumbents, the share that consisted of surplus jobs is higher among the skilled jobs. This is especially the case for start-ups where more than 9 out of 10 new gross jobs involving a long further education were surplus jobs. For incumbent firms it was less than 50%.

[Table 3 around here]

4.4 Industry-Level Results

Table 4 presents a breakdown by 18 different industries (corresponding to the main NACE groups) using our baseline cluster definition. The Table shows considerable heterogeneity across industries. Consider first the numbers for *all firms* in columns 2-4. In this case, the gross-job-creation measure is the sum of the education-specific job creation for all firms within a given industry. Relative to employment in 2002 it varies between 24% (*Financial and insurance*) and 82% (*Human health and social work*), while net job creation relative to employment varies between -15% (*Mining and quarrying*) and 40% (*Travel agent, cleaning and other operational services* and *Human health and social work*). Similarly, surplus job creation relative to employment in 2002 varies between 7% (*Other service activities*) and 46% (*Travel agent, cleaning and other operational services*).

Despite the fact that the three measures of job creation (gross, net and surplus) are strongly positively correlated across industries, there are several industries, where the measures exhibit large absolute and relative differences. A case in point is *Manufacturing*, where almost 25,000 jobs net have been destroyed in the period 2002-2007. Still, more than 30,000 surplus jobs were generated in the same period. In relative terms, this pattern is even more pronounced within *Mining and quarrying*, where net job creation was -349 (corresponding to -15% of the 2002 employment), although 316 surplus jobs were created. Within *Transportation*, net job creation was less than 1% of the initial employment, and still surplus job creation amounted to more than 10% of the employment in 2002. Similar pictures are found within *Information and communication, Financial and insurance*, and *Real estate activities*. In other industries like, *e.g., Construction* and *Accommodation and food service activities*, the net-job-creation measure is much closer to the number of surplus jobs, reflecting that very few jobs were genuinely destroyed in these industries. Hence, relying only on the *NJC* measure is likely to give a distorted picture of the job-creation activity across industries.

[Table 4 around here]

Consider then the relative role of start-ups vs. incumbent firms in the following columns. The role of start-ups in gross job creation varies between 10% (*e.g., Education*) and 45% (*Human health and social work*). When it comes to net job creation, the role of start-ups is even more pronounced with negative contributions from established firms in most industries. However, if we turn to surplus job creation, the established firms play a much more important role. Thus, in more than half of the industries, the established firms dominate when it comes to surplus job creation. This is particularly pronounced within *Education, Financial and insurance* and *Electricity, gas, steam and air conditioning supply*, where incumbent firms were responsible for more than 85% of the surplus jobs, despite the fact that their share in net job creation was "only" around 50%. As opposed to this, in *Other service activities, Accommodation and food service activities* and *Construction*, start-ups accounted for more than 80% of the surplus job creation. This clearly illustrates very diverse contributions of start-ups to job creation across industries.

When it comes to the "newness" of the jobs created by start-ups and incumbents, there are again noticeable differences across industries. In some industries, like *Education* and *Mining and quarrying*, start-ups were only marginally better at creating surplus jobs, while in other industries, like *Construction* and *Knowledge-based services*, start-ups were much more efficient at creating surplus jobs.

In sum, the different industries show distinctively different patterns, and using our measure of surplus job creation allows us to characterize them in more detail than previous studies. Table A1 in the appendix provides a more disaggregate picture of the differences across industries. It is similar to Table 4, but it only aggregates the numbers to 77 industries. This allows us to consider more specific industries, particularly within manufacturing.

5 Robustness Analyses

In this section, we consider the robustness of the results presented in Section 4. Section 5.1 considers the period 2002-2005 to investigate the sensitivity of the results with respect to the time period considered. In Section 5.2, we reproduce the education-, industry- and region-level results from Section 4.3-4.5 using a cluster definition based on 77 industries (corresponding to the 2-digit NACE level) instead of the 233 industries used above (the 3-digit NACE level). Finally, in Section 5.3, we reproduce the education- and industry-level results from Section 4.3 and 4.4 using a cluster definition without the regional dimension included.

5.1 Job Creation, 2002-2005

Table A2 in the appendix presents aggregate results for different cluster definitions when using the period 2002-2005 instead. The numbers in the Table are directly comparable to those in Table 2.

First, note that total net job creation is considerably lower than in Table 2 (33,263 jobs vs. 148,787 jobs). Thus, the 2002-2005 period is less affected by the boom in the Danish economy than the period 2002-2007. It may in that sense be considered to be more representative. Not surprisingly, the lower total net job creation reflects both more negative net job creation by incumbents (- 96,256) and less positive net job creation by start-ups (129,519).

Second, gross job creation is also lower for both types of firms, but as in Table 2 it increases for incumbent firms with the number of education groups used. More interestingly, the start-ups' share of gross job creation is again relatively robust across cluster definitions and still equals approximately a quarter of the total gross job creation.

Third, surplus job creation is also less than in Table 2. Furthermore, for our baseline cluster definition, the absolute difference between total surplus job creation and total net job creation is very similar to that in Table 2. However, the relative difference is now much larger, given that net job creation between 2002 and 2005 was only around 33,000. This further illustrates that the traditional net-job-creation measure is likely to ignore important aspects of the job-creation process.

Fourth, as in Table 2, surplus job creation by incumbent firms increases with the number of clusters used, whereas we again find that surplus job creation by start-ups is much less affected by this. As a consequence, we again find that start-ups accounted for between 40% and 65% of the surplus job creation.

Finally, Table A2 shows that the newness of the jobs created by start-ups is in the range of 50% to 57% for cluster choices in the neighbourhood of our baseline cluster definition. This is slightly lower than in Table 2, which may be a consequence of the lower overall job growth. Similarly, the newness of jobs created by incumbents is also slightly lower than in Table 2.

In sum, using the period 2002-2005 instead of the period 2002-2007 does not alter the main conclusions. The main difference is that the relative difference between surplus job creation and net job creation becomes even larger when using the 2002-2005 period.

5.2 A Job-Cluster Definition with Fewer Industries

Tables A3 and A4 in the appendix are similar to Tables 3 and 4 above, with the exception that they are based on a cluster definition with 77 industries (corresponding to the 2-digit NACE level) instead of the 233 industries (corresponding to the 3-digit NACE level) used in our baseline cluster definition. Note that using a less detailed industry grouping does not affect the aggregate gross- and net-job-creation measures; only the measure of surplus job creation is affected.

Consider first Table A3 with results for different education groups. Compared to Table 3 above the incumbent firms create fewer surplus jobs, and this is particularly the case when it comes to the low-skilled jobs. Thus, surplus jobs requiring only primary schooling drop by more than a third. This reflects that for established firms the net creation of unskilled jobs in one 3-digit NACE industry are partly counteracted by job destruction within "neighbouring" 3-digit NACE industries within the same region. This is to a much lesser extent the case for high-skilled jobs. In other words, unskilled jobs in established firms are more likely to be moved across related industries than are high-skilled jobs.

Surplus job creation by start-ups is only marginally affected compared to Table 3. It increases slightly for some education groups, while it decreases slightly for other groups. Remember that the surplus job creation by start-ups in a job cluster is their net job creation less any net job destruction by incumbents in the same cluster. The fact that the number of surplus unskilled jobs by start-ups does not decrease when using fewer clusters therefore shows that these jobs were not replacing jobs destroyed by incumbents in closely related industries within the same region. In other words, they seem to be genuinely new jobs.

As a consequence of the above, start-ups' share of surplus jobs increases compared to Table 3, in particularly among the low-skilled groups, where it now exceeds 60%. This reinforces the conclusion from Section 4 that the incumbents' share of surplus jobs is highest among the high-skilled groups. Another consequence of distinguishing between "only" 77 industries is that it lowers the newness of the jobs created by incumbents. Again, this is most pronounced for the low-skilled groups. As an example, in Table 3, 18% of the gross jobs with primary schooling created by incumbents were surplus jobs. This number is now down to 12%.

Table A4 is comparable to Table 4, and the surplus job creation by start-ups in the different industries is also very similar to that reported in Table 4. The largest increase is found within *Construction*, where the number of surplus jobs created by start-ups goes up by 6%, and the largest decrease is found within *Real estate activities*, where it decreases by 21%. Thus, in the latter industry, some of the surplus jobs created by start-ups (in Table 4) were counterbalanced by jobs destroyed by incumbents within neighbouring sub-industries within *Real estate activities*.

For incumbent firms, the number of surplus jobs drops within all industries, reflecting that the overall amount of surplus job creation by incumbents decreases when distinguishing between fewer industries. The largest relative decline is found within *Wholesale and retail trade*, where surplus job creation is almost cut in half. Still, the overall picture is the same as in Table 4.

5.3 A Job-Cluster Definition without the Regional Dimension

Tables A5 and A6 in the appendix are similar to Tables 3 and 4, respectively, just without the regional dimension in the cluster definition. That is, the surplus jobs are those that are created on top of the destruction of similar jobs in other firms within the same industry – but not necessarily within the same region.

Not surprisingly, this reduces the total amount of surplus jobs from 289,213 to 253,299, *i.e.*, by 12%. The reduction is largest among incumbent firms (21%), while the number of surplus jobs is only reduced by 3% among start-ups. As a consequence, omitting the regional dimension in the cluster definition reduces the newness of the jobs created by both incumbents (from 22% to 18%) and start-ups (from 64% to 62%), and it also increases the start-ups' share of surplus job creation from 49% to 54%.

If we compare the education-specific numbers in Table A5 with those from Table 3, we can see that the newness of jobs created by start-ups actually increases for the more skilled categories, while it decreases for the less skilled categories and for incumbent firms. Thus, when we disregard the regional dimension of the cluster definition, more of the high-skilled jobs created by start-ups are considered to be surplus jobs, which in turn must reflect more netting out of high-skilled job creation and destruction among established firms in the same industry but in different regions. This is also reflected in the aggregate numbers (column 4), where surplus job creation decreases more for the low-skilled groups. Still, the general insight and conclusions from Section 4.3 remain unchanged.

The same can be said about the industry-specific numbers in Tables A6 and 4. Surplus job creation decreases for all industries, and mostly among incumbent firms. For start-ups, surplus job creation actually increases in some industries, *e.g.*, *Knowledge-based services* and *Information and communication*, but not enough to change the conclusions from Section 4.4.

In sum, omitting the regional dimension in the cluster definition reduces surplus job creation by 12% – but mostly among incumbent firms, and less so in the high-skilled groups. Still, the changes are relatively small, and therefore the insights and conclusions from Section 4 carry through.

6 Surplus Job Creation and Average Wages

We have interpreted surplus jobs as being jobs that are new to a local labour market and hence new to the economy, but so far, we have not looked at whether these jobs are more or less productive or more innovative than other jobs. To get a first impression of this, we can try to compare the quality of jobs in clusters with surplus job creation to the quality of jobs in clusters without surplus job creation. As we cannot identify the individual "surplus job" within a cluster with surplus job creation, one way to do this is to compare and analyse the development in average wages in clusters with and without surplus job creation, respectively.

In this section, we therefore decompose the increase in the average wages following the decomposition techniques suggested by Griliches and Regev (1995) and Foster *et al.* (2001). By decomposing the development in average wages, we can also compare the importance of start-ups and incumbents for the wage development in the two types of clusters.[15]

6.1 Decomposition technique

Our starting point is the decomposition techniques developed by Griliches and Reveg (1995) and Foster *et al.* (2001), and later used by, *e.g.*, Foster *et al.* (2008). We deviate by using wages instead of productivity and by measuring them at the cluster level instead of at the establishment or firm level.

---

[15] It could be argued that it would be more relevant to focus on productivity rather than wages. However, since a firm can be "located" in a number of different clusters – one for each of the educational types that we use – it is impossible to use firm-level productivity measures to compare the productivity of jobs in different clusters. Instead, we have to rely on average wages, as these can be measured at the cluster level.

Formally, the overall average wage, W_t, in year t is given by:

$$W_t = \sum_{j=1}^{n_t} \theta_{j,t} w_{j,t}$$

where $w_{j,t}$ is the average wage rate in sub-cluster j in year t, and $\theta_{j,t}$ is the share of sub-cluster j in total employment in year t. A sub-cluster consists of all jobs within a cluster that belong to a particular type of firm, e.g., a new firm or an established firm, and n_t is the total number of sub-clusters in year t. The change in the overall average wage between $t-5$ and t is then given by:

$$\Delta W_t = W_t - W_{t-5} = \sum_{j=1}^{n_t} \theta_{j,t} w_{j,t} - \sum_{j=1}^{n_{t-5}} \theta_{j,t-5} w_{j,t-5}$$

In the following, we decompose this overall wage change into two parts: one that is due to clusters with "surplus job creation", $\Delta W_{t,SJC\geq 0}$, and one that is due to clusters without surplus job creation, $\Delta W_{t,SJC=0}$. More precisely, we distinguish between four cluster types: (i) clusters with surplus job creation that existed in both $t-5$ and t; (ii) clusters with surplus job creation, which are new and hence only existed in t; (iii) clusters without surplus job creation that existed in both $t-5$ and t; and (iv) clusters without surplus job creation, which only existed in $t-5$, i.e., where all the original jobs were destroyed between $t-5$ and t.[16] Within these clusters, we identify sub-clusters defined by three firm types: (a) incumbents firms, i.e., firms alive in both $t-5$ and t; (b) new (or entering) firms, i.e., firms alive only in the last year, t; and (c) exiting firms, i.e., firms alive only in the initial year, $t-5$.[17]

The overall wage change can then be decomposed as follows:

$$\Delta W_t = \Delta W_{t,SJC\geq 0} + \Delta W_{t,SJC=0}$$

where:

$$\Delta W_{t,SJC\geq 0} = \sum_{j\in i.a} \bar{\theta}_j \Delta w_{j,t} + \sum_{j\in i.a} \Delta \theta_{j,t}(\bar{w}_i - W_{t-5}) + \sum_{j\in ii.a} \theta_{j,t}(w_{j,t} - W_{t-5})$$
$$+ \sum_{j\in i.b} \theta_{j,t}(w_{j,t} - W_{t-5}) + \sum_{j\in ii.b} \theta_{j,t}(w_{j,t} - W_{t-5}) - \sum_{j\in i.c} \theta_{j,t-5}(w_{j,t-5} - W_{t-5})$$

---

[16] By definition we cannot have clusters with surplus job creation that only existed in $t-5$, and clusters without that existed only in t.

[17] Note that by definition not all three firm types can be present in all four cluster types. As an example, we cannot have new firms (type b) in clusters that only existed in $t-5$ (type iv).

and:

$$\Delta W_{t,SJC=0} = \sum_{j \in iii.a} \bar{\theta}_j \Delta w_{j,t} + \sum_{j \in iii.a} \Delta \theta_{j,t}(\bar{w}_j - W_{t-5}) - \sum_{j \in iv.a} \theta_{j,t-5}(w_{j,t-5} - W_{t-5})$$
$$+ \sum_{j \in iii.b} \theta_{j,t}(w_{j,t} - W_{t-5}) - \sum_{j \in iii.c} \theta_{j,t-k}(w_{j,t-5} - W_{t-5}) - \sum_{j \in iv.c} \theta_{j,t-k}(w_{j,t-5} - W_{t-5})$$

A bar above a variable indicates an average of the values in t and $t-5$, e.g., $\bar{w}_j = (w_{j,t} + w_{j,t-5})/2$, whereas the subscripts under the summation sign refer to the sub-clusters defined above. Thus, "$j \in i.a$" means that the summation is done over all sub-clusters j that belong in clusters of type i (clusters with surplus job creation, and which existed in both $t-5$ and t) and consist of firms of type a (incumbent firms).

The first term on the right-hand side in both of the expressions above is the so-called "within-group effect". In the expression for $\Delta W_{t,SJC\geq 0}$, it is the contribution to the change in the average wage from wage changes in incumbent firms in clusters with surplus job creation. It is calculated as the wage changes in these sub-clusters, $\Delta w_{j,t} = w_{j,t} - w_{j,t-5}$, weighted by their average shares in the economy $\bar{\theta}_j = (\theta_{j,t} + \theta_{j,t-5})/2$. In the expression for $\Delta W_{t,SJC=0}$, the interpretation is similar except that we are now looking at the clusters without surplus job creation.

The second term in both expressions is the "between-group effect", which gives the contribution from incumbent firms expanding or contracting their share in employment in clusters with (or without) surplus job creation. It is calculated as the changes in the market shares of the relevant sub-clusters multiplied by the difference between the sub-clusters average wage and the economy-wide average wage in $t-5$. Thus, if wages are higher in a sub-cluster than the initial overall average, and the sub-cluster expands, then this term will contribute to an increase in the average wage.

The third term in the first expression is the contribution from incumbent firms opening up jobs in new clusters, i.e., clusters that did not exist in $t-5$. If these jobs have wages that are higher than the initial economy-wide average, W_{t-5}, this term will be positive. Similarly, in the second expression, the third term expresses the contribution from incumbent firms closing down jobs in clusters that disappear between $t-5$ and t. If the wages of these closing jobs were lower than the economy-wide average, W_{t-5}, this term will be positive.

The remaining terms measure the contributions from entering and exiting firms. In the first expression, the fourth and fifth terms represent contributions from entering firms in clusters with surplus job creation that existed (the fourth term) and did not exist (the fifth term), respectively, in $t-5$. If these entering firms have higher wages than the initial economy-wide average, W_{t-5}, these terms become positive. Similarly, the fourth term in the second expression is the contribution from entering firms in clusters without surplus job creation. By definition, these clusters all existed in $t-5$.

The last term in the first expression is an exit effect. It gives the contribution from exiting firms in clusters with surplus job creation. By definition, these clusters were all "alive" in $t-5$. If the exiting firms had lower wages than the average, this term will be positive. In the second expression, there are two terms representing the contributions from exiting firms: In clusters that remained present in t (the fifth term) and in clusters that closed before t (the sixth term). In both cases, lower wages of the exiting firms will serve to make these terms positive.

Note that the decomposition presented above follows Foster *et al.* (2001). If we were to follow Griliches and Regev (1995), W_{t-5} should be replaced by $\overline{W}$ throughout in the expressions above. Thus, in Foster et al. (2001), the contributions of the last five terms are measured relative to the initial average wage, whereas in Griliches and Regev (1995), they are measured relative to the average between $t-5$ and t.

6.2 Results
Table 5 reports the results from the decomposition above, using both the approach of Foster *et al.* (2001), which is referred to as FHK, and the approach of Griliches and Regev (1995), which is referred to as GR. In both cases, we decompose the overall average wage change between 2002 and 2007 (measured in 2002 prices).

The table shows that around two-thirds of the observed increase in the average wage rate can be ascribed to jobs in clusters with surplus job creation (the upper part of the Table) and that the remaining around one third can be ascribed to jobs in clusters without (the lower part). As can be seen form the last two columns, these shares respond roughly to the shares of these clusters in total employment in the final year, but are therefore also higher than their share in employment in the initial year. Thus, there is a (small) tendency for clusters with surplus job creation to contribute relatively more to wage growth than their employment share would suggest.

If we turn to the contributions within these two cluster types, we can see that (by far) the largest contributions come from incumbent and exiting firms. This goes for both cluster types. The contribution from new firms, on the other hand, is at best absent. Using the Foster et al. (2001) approach where wages of new firms are compared with the initial average wage (in 2002), we find no contribution from new firms, whereas we get a slightly negative contribution when using the Griliches and Regev (1995) decomposition method, where wages of new firms are compared with the average of the 2002 and 2007 economy-wide average. This is true for clusters both with and without surplus job creation.

Thus, new firm have wages at or below the average, and there is no sign that new firms contribute more in clusters with surplus job creation. This echoes a common finding in the literature, namely that there is no significant difference between entrants and incumbents in (revenue based) productivity levels; see Foster et al. (2008).

[Table 5 around here]

Based on these results, we conclude that the contribution to average wage growth from job clusters with surplus jobs corresponds roughly to their share in employment. We also conclude that the contribution from new firms is at best absent (their jobs are of average quality), and that there are no visible differences between their contributions to clusters with and without surplus job creation.

An obvious limitation of the above decomposition is, of course, that we do not control for worker and firm characteristics in computing the average wages. Thus, it may actually be the case that entrepreneurial firms contribute to average wage growth if they hire, e.g., less-experienced workers to a larger extent than other firms. In that case, a zero contribution to the average wage translates into a positive contribution to the experience-specific wage.

Another important limitation is that entering plants/firms may charge lower prices than incumbents as documented in Foster et al. (2008) for US manufacturing firms producing homogeneous products. If this is the case for Danish entrepreneurs, and wages are determined by the value of the marginal product of labor, then wages will be lower for entrepreneurs than for incumbents that charge higher product prices.

7 Conclusion

In this paper, we extend earlier analyses of the job creation of start-ups vs. established firms by taking into consideration the educational content of the jobs created and destroyed. More specifically, we define education-specific measures of job creation and job destruction at the firm level. This results in higher firm-level gross job creation than the traditional measure of gross job creation from the literature, as it takes into account that a firm might simultaneously create, say, skilled jobs while it destructs unskilled jobs. This is not captured by the traditional measure. More specifically, using Danish data from 2002-2007 that cover almost the entire Danish private sector, we find that overall gross job creation increases by more than 8% if we distinguish between 7 educational groups, and with more than 12% if we distinguish between 32 educational groups compared to the case where we use the traditional measure.

Furthermore, our education-specific measure of job creation allows us to introduce and construct a measure of "surplus job creation" defined as jobs created on top of any simultaneous destruction of highly similar jobs, *i.e.*, jobs within the same educational group in established firms in the same region and industry. We can think of this as jobs added to a "local labour market" defined by skill, region and industry. Distinguishing between seven educational groups, 233 industries and five regions, we find that the creation of surplus jobs is almost twice the net job creation in the economy in the period 2002-2007, and if we consider the period 2002-2005, the relative difference is even larger. In other words, relying on the traditional measures of gross and net job creation hides a lot of important job-market dynamics.

Our data also allow us to identify the organic start-ups (nascent firms). Combined with our education-specific measure of job creation and our measure of surplus job creation, this enables us to analyse the role of start-up firms in the job-creation process at a much more detailed level than previous studies.

Our analysis shows that a large share of the net job creation in start-ups is counterbalanced by the destruction of similar jobs in incumbent firms. Although our analysis does not reveal the direction of causality, it strongly indicates that the contribution of start-ups to job creation might be less than revealed by the traditional measures. Thus, while start-ups can account for the entire net job creation, they "only" create approximately half of the surplus jobs. In other words, incumbent firms play a significant role in adding new jobs to the "local labour markets".

Furthermore, our approach allows us to characterize and identify differences across industries, education groups and regions. We find, *e.g.*, that start-ups create a larger share of the surplus low-skilled jobs. Furthermore, our findings show that a larger share of the high-skilled jobs created tends to be surplus jobs – especially when created by start-ups.

Our results also show large differences across industries – both in terms of job creation and when it comes to the relative role of start-ups vs. incumbent firms. In some industries, such as *Education*, *Financial and insurance* and *Electricity, gas, steam and air conditioning supply*, incumbent firms are responsible for more than 85% of surplus job creation, despite the fact that their share in net job creation is "only" around 50%. In contrast, in industries such as *Other service activities*, *Accomodation and food service activities*, and *Construction*, start-ups account for more than 80% of the surplus jobs.

In sum, this paper sheds new light on the job creation and job destruction paper. It documents the importance of simultaneous job creation and destruction of different types of jobs within firms, and that established firms contribute significantly to the creation of additional jobs at locally defined labour markets. It also shows that many of the jobs created by start-ups reflect the destruction of similar jobs in established firms. Thus, start-ups might to some extent be crowding out economic activity of established firms or, alternatively, they might simply inherit market shares of other firms that are closing down (for whatever reason) rather than driving them out of the market.

The question of what comes first – destruction of jobs in established firms or creation of jobs in start-ups – is outside the scope of the present analysis, but it remains an obvious question for further research. At this point, we note that there is simultaneity of job creation and destruction, which advises us to be aware of potential negative externalities of job creation in start-ups on the job creation of established firms.

References

Acs, Z., & Audretsch, D. (1990): *Innovation and Small Firms*. Cambridge, MA: MIT Press.

Agarwal, R. (1998): "Small Firm Survival and Technological Activity", *Small Business Economics,* 11, 215-224.

Audretsch, D. (1995): *Innovation and Industry Evolution*. Cambridge, MA: MIT Press.

Audretsch, D., & Fritsch, M. (2002): "Growth Regimes over Time and Space", *Regional Studies*, 36, 113-124.

Baldwin, J., & Picot, G. (1995): "Employment Generation by Small Producers in the Canadian Manufacturing Sector", *Small Business Economics*, 7, 317-331.

Barnes, M. & Haskel, J. (2002): "Job Creation, Job Destruction and the Contribution of Small Businesses: Evidence for UK Manufacturing", University of London Queen Mary Economics Working Paper No. 461.

Bartelsman, E., Haltiwanger, J.C., & Scarpetta, S. (2004). Microeconomic evidence of creative destruction in industrial and developing countries. IZA Discussion Paper No. 1374. Institute for the Study of Labor (IZA), Bonn

Birch, D. (1981): "Who Creates Jobs?", *The Public Interest*, 65, 3-14.

Birch, D. (1987): *Job Creation in America*. New York and London: The Free Press.

Broersma, L. & Gautier, P. (1997): "Job Creation and Job Destruction by Small Firms: An Empirical Investigation for the Dutch Manufacturing Sector", *Small Business Economics*, 9, 211-224.

Davis, S.J., & Haltiwanger, J. (1992): "Gross job creation, gross job destruction and employment reallocation", *Quarterly Journal of Economics*, 107, 819-863.

Davis, S.J., Haltiwanger, J. & Schuh, S. (1996a). *Job Creation and Destruction*. Cambridge, MA: MIT Press.

Davis, S.J., Haltiwanger, J. & Schuh, S. (1996b): "Small Business and Job Creation: Dissecting the Myth and Reassessing the Facts", *Small Business Economics*, 8, 297-315.

Dosi, G. (1982): "Technological Paradigms and Technological Trajectories: A Suggested Interpretation of the Determinants and Directions of Technical Change", *Research Policy*, 11, 147-162.

Dosi, G. (1988): "Sources, Procedures, and Microeconomic Effects of Innovation", *Journal of Economic Literature*", 26, 1120-1171.

Dunne, T., Haltiwanger, J. & Troske, K.R. (1997): "Technology and Jobs: Secular Changes and Cyclical Dynamics", *Carnegie-Rochester Conference Series on Public Policy*, 46, 107-178.

Dunne, T., Roberts, M., & Samuelson, L. (1989): "The Growth and Failures of U.S. Manufacturing Establishments", *Quarterly Journal of Economics*, 104, 671-698.

Foster, L.S., Haltiwanger, J.C. & Krizan, C.J. (2001). Aggregate productivity growth: Lessons from microeconomic evidence. In E. Dean, M. Harper, & C. Hulten (Eds.), New developments in productivity analysis. Chicago: University of Chicago Press.

Foster, L., Haltiwanger, J. & Syverson, C. (2008), "Reallocation, Firm Turnover, and Efficiency: Selection on Productivity or Profitability?", *American Economic Review*, 98, 394-425.

Fölster, S. (2000): "Do Entrepreneurs Create Jobs?", *Small Business Economics*, 14, 137-148.

Fritsch, M., & Mueller, P. (2008): "The Effect of New Business Formation on Regional Development over Time: The Case of Germany", *Small Business Economics*, 30, 15-29.

Gort, M. & Klepper, S. (1982): "Time Paths in the Diffusion of Product Innovations", *Economic Journal*, 92, 630-653.

Griliches, Z, & Regev, H. (1995), "Firm Productivity in Isaeli Industry: 1979-1988", *Journal of Econometrics*, 65(1), 197-203

Haltiwanger, J., Jarmin, R., & Miranda, J. (2013): "Who Creates Jobs? Small versus Large versus Young", *Review of Economics and Statistics*, 95, 347-361.

Hohti, S. (2000): "Job Flows and Job Quality by Establishment Size in the Finnish Manufacturing Sector 1980-94", *Small Business Economics*, 15, 265-281.

Klette, T., & Mathiassen, A. (1996): "Job Creation, Job Destruction and Establishment Turnover in Norwegian Manufacturing", *Annales d'Economie et de Statistique*, 41/42, 97-125.

Malchow-Møller, N., Schjerning, B., & Sørensen, A. (2011): "Entrepreneurship, Job Creation and Wage Growth", *Small Business Economics*, 36, 15-32.

Malerba, F. (1992): "Learning by Firms and Incremental Technical Change", *Economic Journal*, 102, 845-859.

Malerba, F., & Orsenigo, L. (1993): "Technological Regimes and Firm Behavior", *Industrial and Corporate Change*, 2, 45-71.

Nelson, R., & Winter, S. (1982): *An Evolutionary Theory of Economic Change*. Cambridge, MA: Harvard University Press.

Neumark, D., Wall, B., & Zhang, J. (2011). "Do Small Businesses Create More Jobs? New Evidence for the United States from the National Establishment Time Series", *Review of Economics and Statistics*, 93, 16-29.

Neumark, D., Zhang, J., & Wall, B. (2006): "Where the Jobs are: Business Dynamics and Employment Growth", *Academy of Management Perspectives*, 20, 79–94.

Shane, S. (2009): "Why Encouraging More People to Become Entrepreneurs is Bad Public Policy", *Small Business Economics*, 33, 141-149.

Spletzer, J. (2000): "The Contribution of Establishment Births and Deaths to Employment Growth", *Journal of Business and Economic Statistics*, 18, 113-126.

Stevens, M. (1994): "A Theoretical Model of On-the-Job Training with Imperfect Competition", *Oxford Economic Papers*, 46, 537-562.

Stevens, M. (1996): "Transferable Training and Poaching Externalities", in A. Booth, & D. Snower (eds.), *Acquiring skills*, Cambridge University Press, 21-40.

Wagner, J. (1994): "The Post-Entry Performance of New Small Firms in German Manufacturing Industries", *Journal of Industrial Economics*, 42, 141-154.

Wagner, J. (1995): "Firm Size and Job Creation in Germany", *Small Business Economics*, 7, 469-474.

Winter, S.G. (1984): "Schumpeterian Competition in Alternative Technological Regimes", *Journal of Economic Behavior & Organization*, 5, 287-320.

Table 1. Aggregate Gross and Net Job Creation, 2002-2007

	Number of education groups	Employment in 2002	All firms			Incumbent firms		Start-up firms		Start-ups' share of:
			GJC_A	GJD_A	NJC_A	GJC_A^{in}	NJC_A^{in}	GJC_A^{su}	NJC_A^{su}	GJC_A
(1)	1	1,797,472	814,594	665,807	148,787	596,535	-69,272	218,059	218,059	0.268
(2)	7	1,797,472	883,117	734,330	148,787	665,058	-69,272	218,059	218,059	0.247
(3)	32	1,797,472	915,316	766,529	148,787	697,257	-69,272	218,059	218,059	0.238

Note: See text for definitions of the different education-specific job-creation and job-destruction measures.

Table 2. Surplus Job Creation, 2002-2007, Baseline Cluster Definition and Alternative Cluster Definitions

	# clusters	# industries	# regions	# education groups	All firms SJC_A	GJC_A	NJC_A	Incumbent firms SJC_A^{in}	GJC_A^{in}	NJC_A^{in}	Start-up firms SJC_A^{su}	GJC_A^{su}	NJC_A^{su}	Start-ups' share of: GJC_A	SJC_A	Newness of jobs by: start-ups	incumbents
(1)	7,175	233	5	7	289,213	883,117	148,787	148,933	665,058	-69,272	140,280	218,059	218,059	0.247	0.485	0.64	0.22
(2)	35	1	5	7	157,347	883,117	148,787	38,434	665,058	-69,272	118,913	218,059	218,059	0.247	0.756	0.55	0.06
(3)	630	18	5	7	213,881	883,117	148,787	74,007	665,058	-69,272	139,874	218,059	218,059	0.247	0.654	0.64	0.11
(4)	2,585	77	5	7	248,548	883,117	148,787	108,301	665,058	-69,272	140,247	218,059	218,059	0.247	0.564	0.64	0.16
(5)	7,175	233	5	7	289,213	883,117	148,787	148,933	665,058	-69,272	140,280	218,059	218,059	0.247	0.485	0.64	0.22
(6)	17,532	617	5	7	341,212	883,117	148,787	204,426	665,058	-69,272	136,786	218,059	218,059	0.247	0.401	0.63	0.31
(7)	1,094	233	5	1	258,919	814,594	148,787	111,708	596,535	-69,272	147,211	218,059	218,059	0.268	0.569	0.68	0.19
(8)	7,175	233	5	7	289,213	883,117	148,787	148,933	665,058	-69,272	140,280	218,059	218,059	0.247	0.485	0.64	0.22
(9)	23,332	233	5	32	305,302	915,316	148,787	166,891	697,257	-69,272	138,411	218,059	218,059	0.238	0.453	0.63	0.24
(10)	1,597	233	1	7	253,299	883,117	148,787	117,037	665,058	-69,272	136,262	218,059	218,059	0.247	0.538	0.62	0.18
(11)	7,175	233	5	7	289,213	883,117	148,787	148,933	665,058	-69,272	140,280	218,059	218,059	0.247	0.485	0.64	0.22
(12)	13,781	233	12	7	320,788	883,117	148,787	180,550	665,058	-69,272	140,238	218,059	218,059	0.247	0.437	0.64	0.27
(13)	1	1	1	1	148,787	814,594	148,787	0	596,535	-69,272	148,787	218,059	218,059	0.268	1.000	0.68	0.00
(14)	80,221	617	12	32	408,447	915,316	148,787	270,000	697,257	-69,272	138,447	218,059	218,059	0.238	0.339	0.63	0.39

Note: Row 1 uses the baseline definition of a job cluster with seven education groups, five regions and 233 industries, while rows 2-14 use alternative job-cluster definitions. See text for definitions of the different education-specific job-creation and job-destruction measures.

TABLE 3. Job Creation by Education Groups, 2002-2007, Baseline Cluster Definition

	Employment in 2002	All firms			Incumbent firms			Start-up firms			Start-ups' share of:		Newness of jobs by:	
		GJC_A	NJC_A	SJC_A	GJC_A^{in}	NJC_A^{in}	SJC_A^{in}	GJC_A^{su}	NJC_A^{su}	SJC_A^{su}	GJC_A	SJC_A	start-ups	incumbents
Total	1,797,472	883,117	148,787	289,213	665,058	-69,272	148,933	218,059	218,059	140,280	0.25	0.49	0.64	0.22
By education group:														
Primary schooling	546,646	261,355	22,610	75,175	198,586	-40,159	36,035	62,769	62,769	39,140	0.24	0.52	0.62	0.18
Vocational education	718,244	291,302	16,971	73,180	213,246	-61,085	31,690	78,056	78,056	41,490	0.27	0.57	0.53	0.15
High school	169,680	97,504	18,042	30,563	74,400	-5,062	16,934	23,104	23,104	13,629	0.24	0.45	0.59	0.23
Short further education	83,793	47,704	16,218	20,279	37,529	6,043	12,548	10,175	10,175	7,731	0.21	0.38	0.76	0.33
Medium further education	130,209	74,486	27,488	33,878	56,046	9,048	18,286	18,440	18,440	15,592	0.25	0.46	0.85	0.33
Long further education	80,649	53,490	27,292	29,998	41,505	15,307	19,046	11,985	11,985	10,952	0.22	0.37	0.91	0.46
Unknown	68,251	57,276	20,166	26,140	43,746	6,636	14,394	13,530	13,530	11,746	0.24	0.45	0.87	0.33

Note: Baseline cluster definition used. See text for definitions of the different education-specific job-creation and job-destruction measures.

TABLE 4. Job Creation by Industry Groups, 2002-2007, Baseline Cluster Definition

	Employment in 2002	All firms			Incumbent firms			Start-up firms			Start-ups' share of:			Newness of jobs by:	
		GJC_A	NJC_A	SJC_A	GJC_A^{in}	NJC_A^{in}	SJC_A^{in}	GJC_A^{su}	NJC_A^{su}	SJC_A^{su}	GJC_A	SJC_A		start-ups	incumbents
Total	1,797,472	883,117	148,787	289,213	665,058	-69,272	148,933	218,059	218,059	140,280	0.25	0.49		0.64	0.22
By industry:															
Wholesale and retail trade	421,920	229,266	41,275	60,232	187,358	-633	32,584	41,908	41,908	27,648	0.18	0.46		0.66	0.17
Manufacturing	415,629	110,995	-24,496	31,750	95,458	-40,033	24,894	15,537	15,537	6,856	0.14	0.22		0.44	0.26
Construction	172,067	98,796	30,902	32,718	62,094	-5,800	6,289	36,702	36,702	26,429	0.37	0.81		0.72	0.10
Transportation	153,038	63,391	872	16,666	48,150	-14,369	8,323	15,241	15,241	8,343	0.24	0.50		0.55	0.17
Knowledge-based services	118,980	70,092	21,447	26,882	47,057	-1,588	8,993	23,035	23,035	17,889	0.33	0.67		0.78	0.19
Travel agent, cleaning and other operational services	109,030	85,775	44,108	50,571	65,679	24,012	35,521	20,096	20,096	15,050	0.23	0.30		0.75	0.54
Information and communication	95,426	56,648	2,704	14,992	44,396	-9,548	7,955	12,252	12,252	7,037	0.22	0.47		0.57	0.18
Accomodation and food service activities	89,428	65,471	16,166	17,381	39,884	-9,421	2,508	25,587	25,587	14,873	0.39	0.86		0.58	0.06
Financial and insurance	79,209	19,218	-659	8,813	17,154	-2,723	7,550	2,064	2,064	1,263	0.11	0.14		0.61	0.44
Education	30,009	13,509	4,334	4,998	12,189	3,014	4,383	1,320	1,320	615	0.10	0.12		0.47	0.36
Other service activities	29,145	14,980	-1,368	1,977	9,221	-7,127	257	5,759	5,759	1,720	0.38	0.87		0.30	0.03
Real estate activities	27,947	16,568	-572	3,726	10,732	-6,408	1,290	5,836	5,836	2,436	0.35	0.65		0.42	0.12
Arts, entertainment and other services	17,711	12,086	5,342	5,629	8,563	1,819	2,897	3,523	3,523	2,732	0.29	0.49		0.78	0.34
Human health and social work	17,443	14,368	6,945	7,458	7,881	458	2,037	6,487	6,487	5,421	0.45	0.73		0.84	0.26
Electricity, gas, steam and air conditioning supply	8,871	5,790	1,043	2,439	5,214	467	2,095	576	576	344	0.10	0.14		0.60	0.40
Water supply, sewerage and waste management	7,867	2,762	-481	963	2,480	-763	773	282	282	190	0.10	0.20		0.67	0.31
Mining and quarrying	2,294	664	-349	316	458	-555	196	206	206	120	0.31	0.38		0.58	0.43
Activity not stated	1,458	2,738	1,574	1,702	1,090	-74	388	1,648	1,648	1,314	0.60	0.77		0.80	0.36

Note: Baseline cluster definition used. See text for definitions of the different education-specific job-creation and job-destruction measures.

TABLE 5. Decomposition of the increase in average wages, 2002–2007

	(FHK)	(GR)	2002	2007
	Wage increase in DKK		Employment shares	
	10.18	10.18	100%	100%
SJC>0	68.2%	63.0%	58%	68%
Incumbents - within effect	44.3%	44.3%	45%	62%
Incumbents - between effect	11.6%	3.2%	-	0%
Incumbents, new clusters	0.1%	0.0%	-	7%
Entry, existing clusters	-0.1%	-3.4%	-	0%
Entry, new clusters	0.0%	0.0%	13%	-
Exit, existing clusters	12.4%	18.8%		
SJC=0	31.7%	36.9%	42%	32%
Incumbents - within effect	29.4%	29.4%	31%	30%
Incumbents - between effect	-2.8%	-2.2%	-	-
Incumbents, closing clusters	0.0%	0.0%	0%	2%
Entry	-0.5%	-1.2%	-	-
Exit, existing clusters	5.7%	11.0%	11%	-
Exit, closing clusters	-0.2%	-0.1%	0%	-

Note: This table shows decompositons of wage increase for the private sector using the two decomposition methods referred to in the text. The first column labelled "Wage increase" reflects the average weighted five year wage increase. The first row present the average increase in DKK (Danish kroner); the remaining rows present the contribution - in percent - of the individual terms in the decomposition. The aggregate consumption price index was used as price deflator. Wages are measured in 2002 prices. The calculations are performed for 15.861 sub-clusters. The second column labelled "employment shares" present the shares of total employment in the different sub-cluster types. FHK is calculated using the approach of Foster et al. (2001), whereas GR is calculated using the approach of Griliches and Gegev (1995).

Appendix

[Table A1 around here]

[Table A2 around here]

[Table A3 around here]

[Table A4 around here]

[Table A5 around here]

[Table A6 around here]

TABLE A1. Job Creation by Industry Groups, 2002-2007, Baseline Cluster Definition

	Employment in 2002	All firms			Incumbent firms			Start-up firms			Start-ups' share of:			Newness of jobs by:	
		GJC_A	NJC_A	SJC_A	GJC_A^{in}	NJC_A^{in}	SJC_A^{in}	GJC_A^{su}	NJC_A^{su}	SJC_A^{su}	GJC_A	NJC_A	SC_A	*start-ups*	*incumbents*
Total	1,781,100	878,464	151,441	287,768	661,650	-65,373	148,249	216,814	216,814	139,519	0.25	1.43	0.48	0.64	0.22
By industry:															
Extraction of crude petroleum and natural gas															
Other mining and quarrying	1,421	459	33	199	321	-105	132	138	138	67	0.30	4.18	0.34	0.49	0.41
Mining support service activities	761	190	-369	115	122	-437	62	68	68	53	0.36	-0.18	0.46	0.78	0.51
Manufacture of food products	75,620	15,070	-11,604	2,324	12,104	-14,570	1,640	2,966	2,966	684	0.20	-0.26	0.29	0.23	0.14
Manufacture of beverages	5,528	720	-566	430	452	-834	301	268	268	129	0.37	-0.47	0.30	0.48	0.67
Manufacture of tobacco products															
Manufacture of textiles	6,465	1,628	-984	220	1,333	-1,279	131	295	295	89	0.18	-0.30	0.40	0.30	0.10
Manufacture of wearing apparel	4,165	1,055	-974	183	852	-1,177	107	203	203	76	0.19	-0.21	0.42	0.37	0.13
Manufacture of leather and related products															
Manufacture of wood and of products of wood and cork etc.	15,505	5,020	178	1,378	4,339	-503	904	681	681	474	0.14	3.83	0.34	0.70	0.21
Manufacture of paper and paper products															
Printing and reproduction of recorded media	14,371	3,616	-3,399	196	2,958	-4,057	148	658	658	48	0.18	-0.19	0.24	0.07	0.05
Manufacture of coke and refined petroleum products															
Manufacture of chemicals and chemical products	14,584	2,134	-2,105	914	1,956	-2,283	841	178	178	73	0.08	-0.08	0.08	0.41	0.43
Manufacture of basic pharmaceutical products and pharmaceutical preparations	15,688	2,962	1,354	2,033	2,909	1,301	2,000	53	53	33	0.02	0.04	0.02	0.62	0.69
Manufacture of rubber and plastic products	23,712	5,784	-1,456	960	5,384	-1,856	848	400	400	112	0.07	-0.27	0.12	0.28	0.16
Manufacture of other non-metallic mineral products	18,240	5,145	649	2,261	4,699	203	1,982	446	446	279	0.09	0.69	0.12	0.63	0.42
Manufacture of basic metals	6,610	1,828	-370	1,024	1,597	-601	930	231	231	94	0.13	-0.62	0.09	0.41	0.58
Manufacture of fabricated metal products, except machinery and equipment	42,033	15,866	2,593	4,655	12,640	-633	2,560	3,226	3,226	2,095	0.20	1.24	0.45	0.65	0.20
Manufacture of computer, electronic and optical products	22,400	6,672	-920	2,612	6,348	-1,244	2,390	324	324	222	0.05	-0.35	0.08	0.69	0.38
Manufacture of electrical equipment	15,522	4,023	-2,305	2,179	3,684	-2,644	2,038	339	339	141	0.08	-0.15	0.06	0.42	0.55
Manufacture of machineryand equipment n.e.c.	67,517	19,796	2,019	5,725	17,740	-37	4,326	2,056	2,056	1,399	0.10	1.02	0.24	0.68	0.24
Manufacture of motor vehicles, trailers and semi-trailers	6,446	2,338	284	1,159	2,226	172	1,094	112	112	65	0.05	0.39	0.06	0.58	0.49
Manufacture of other transport equipment	4,752	1,270	496	781	1,146	372	715	124	124	66	0.10	0.25	0.08	0.53	0.62
Manufacture of furniture	16,997	5,137	-879	702	4,990	-1,026	621	147	147	81	0.03	-0.17	0.12	0.55	0.12
Other manufacturing	13,371	2,962	-1,391	812	2,315	-2,038	509	647	647	303	0.22	-0.47	0.37	0.47	0.22
Repair and installation of machinery and equipment	14,826	6,621	-1,454	1,011	4,563	-3,512	624	2,058	2,058	387	0.31	-1.42	0.38	0.19	0.14
Electricity, gas, steam and air conditioning supply	8,871	5,790	1,043	2,439	5,214	467	2,095	576	576	344	0.10	0.55	0.14	0.60	0.40
Water collection, treatment and supply	1,231	662	111	219	615	64	185	47	47	34	0.07	0.42	0.16	0.72	0.30
Sewerage	1,262	408	166	221	353	111	177	55	55	44	0.13	0.33	0.20	0.80	0.50
Waste collection, treatment and disposal activities; materials recovery	5,269	1,681	-664	516	1,512	-833	411	169	169	105	0.10	-0.25	0.20	0.62	0.27
Remediation activities and other waste management services															
Construction of buildings	33,244	17,063	3,647	5,253	10,380	-3,036	965	6,683	6,683	4,288	0.39	1.83	0.82	0.64	0.09
Civil engineering	12,862	6,309	3,451	3,582	4,485	1,627	1,841	1,824	1,824	1,741	0.29	0.53	0.49	0.95	0.41
Specialised construction activities	125,961	75,424	23,804	23,883	47,229	-4,391	3,483	28,195	28,195	20,400	0.37	1.18	0.85	0.72	0.07
Wholesale and retail trade and repair of motor vehicles and motorcycles	49,558	24,986	5,979	6,598	20,124	1,117	3,356	4,862	4,862	3,242	0.19	0.81	0.49	0.67	0.17
Wholesale trade, except of motor vehicles and motorcycles	167,586	76,963	11,163	19,801	64,135	-1,665	12,682	12,828	12,828	7,119	0.17	1.15	0.36	0.55	0.20
Retail trade, except of motor vehicles and motorcycles	204,776	127,317	24,133	33,833	103,099	-85	16,546	24,218	24,218	17,287	0.19	1.00	0.51	0.71	0.16
Land transport and transport via pipelines	74,812	34,322	2,586	4,712	26,646	-5,090	2,250	7,676	7,676	2,462	0.22	2.97	0.52	0.32	0.08
Water transport	9,009	3,595	-1,372	883	2,755	-2,212	348	840	840	535	0.23	-0.61	0.61	0.64	0.13
Air transport	11,656	3,736	-5,758	335	3,578	-5,916	274	158	158	61	0.04	-0.03	0.18	0.39	0.08
Warehousing and support activities for transportation	24,149	13,726	5,542	6,069	12,193	4,009	4,760	1,533	1,533	1,309	0.11	0.28	0.22	0.85	0.39
Postal and courier activities	33,412	8,012	-126	4,667	2,978	-5,160	691	5,034	5,034	3,976	0.63	-39.95	0.85	0.79	0.23
Accommodation	20,886	11,017	1,933	2,691	8,626	-458	1,411	2,391	2,391	1,280	0.22	1.24	0.48	0.54	0.16
Food and beverage service activities	68,542	54,454	14,233	14,690	31,258	-8,963	1,097	23,196	23,196	13,593	0.43	1.63	0.93	0.59	0.04
Publishing activities	24,833	9,753	-1,404	3,871	8,367	-2,790	3,343	1,386	1,386	528	0.14	-0.99	0.14	0.38	0.40
Motion picture, video and television programme production etc.	7,156	4,737	1,294	1,664	3,199	-244	1,062	1,538	1,538	602	0.32	1.19	0.36	0.39	0.33
Programming and broadcasting activities	2,336	1,074	410	691	909	245	621	165	165	70	0.15	0.40	0.10	0.42	0.68
Telecommunications	21,592	14,585	-3,784	1,949	13,956	-4,413	1,684	629	629	265	0.04	-0.17	0.14	0.42	0.12
Computer programming, consultancy and related activities	36,106	24,027	5,457	5,984	16,216	-2,354	869	7,811	7,811	5,115	0.33	1.43	0.85	0.65	0.05
Information service activities															
Financial service activities, except insurance and pension funding	56,216	13,794	2,143	7,265	12,270	619	6,287	1,524	1,524	978	0.11	0.71	0.13	0.64	0.51
Insurance, reinsurance and pension funding, except compulsorysocial security	18,323	3,195	-3,378	644	3,090	-3,483	616	105	105	28	0.03	-0.03	0.04	0.27	0.20
Activities auxiliary to financial services and insurance activities	4,670	2,229	576	904	1,794	141	647	435	435	257	0.20	0.76	0.28	0.59	0.36
Real estate activities	27,947	16,568	-572	3,726	10,732	-6,408	1,290	5,836	5,836	2,436	0.35	-10.20	0.65	0.42	0.12
Legal and accounting activities	29,078	11,982	1,205	3,213	8,885	-1,892	1,417	3,097	3,097	1,796	0.26	2.57	0.56	0.58	0.16
Activities of head offices; management consultancy activities	12,231	15,000	8,087	8,130	7,821	908	1,979	7,179	7,179	6,151	0.48	0.89	0.76	0.86	0.25
Architectural and engineering activities; technical testing and analysis	34,630	17,198	6,395	6,665	12,415	1,612	2,615	4,783	4,783	4,050	0.28	0.75	0.61	0.85	0.21
Scientific research and development	3,904	2,156	742	917	1,509	95	345	647	647	572	0.30	0.87	0.62	0.88	0.23
Advertising and market research	25,838	15,087	3,312	4,678	11,128	-647	1,814	3,959	3,959	2,864	0.26	1.20	0.61	0.72	0.16
Other professional, scientific and technical activities	10,937	7,075	1,119	2,677	4,118	-1,838	568	2,957	2,957	2,109	0.42	2.64	0.79	0.71	0.14
Veterinary activities	2,362	1,594	587	602	1,181	174	255	413	413	347	0.26	0.70	0.58	0.84	0.22
Rental and leasing activities	8,648	4,620	928	1,727	3,492	-200	920	1,128	1,128	807	0.24	1.22	0.47	0.72	0.26
Employment activities	32,765	41,523	31,883	31,914	33,208	23,568	24,083	8,315	8,315	7,831	0.20	0.26	0.25	0.94	0.73
Travel agency, tour operator reservation service and related activities	4,983	2,682	874	1,163	2,185	377	817	497	497	346	0.19	0.57	0.30	0.70	0.37
Security and investigation activities	2,404	3,804	2,878	3,002	2,997	2,071	2,273	807	807	729	0.21	0.28	0.24	0.90	0.76
Services to buildings and landscape activities	49,694	24,078	4,166	7,832	17,211	-2,701	4,242	6,867	6,867	3,590	0.29	1.65	0.46	0.52	0.25
Office administrative, office support and other business support activities	10,536	9,068	3,379	4,933	6,586	897	3,186	2,482	2,482	1,747	0.27	0.73	0.35	0.70	0.48
Education	30,009	13,509	4,334	4,998	12,189	3,014	4,383	1,320	1,320	615	0.10	0.30	0.12	0.47	0.36
Human health activities	17,443	14,368	6,945	7,458	7,881	458	2,037	6,487	6,487	5,421	0.45	0.93	0.73	0.84	0.26
Creative, arts and entertainment activities	3,415	2,269	452	600	1,431	-386	139	838	838	461	0.37	1.85	0.77	0.55	0.10
Libraries, archives, museums and other cultural activities	2,641	1,511	805	884	1,442	736	827	69	69	57	0.05	0.09	0.06	0.83	0.57
Gambling and betting activities															
Sports activities and amusement and recreation activities	10,180	7,499	3,701	3,733	5,269	1,471	1,810	2,230	2,230	1,923	0.30	0.60	0.52	0.86	0.34
Repair of computers and personal and household goods	8,984	3,150	-2,687	410	2,240	-3,597	145	910	910	265	0.29	-0.34	0.65	0.29	0.06
Other personal service activities	20,084	11,808	1,338	1,565	6,961	-3,509	110	4,847	4,847	1,455	0.41	3.62	0.93	0.30	0.02
Activities of extraterritorial organisations and bodies	1,535	2,760	1,555	1,704	1,110	-95	390	1,650	1,650	1,314	0.60	1.06	0.77	0.80	0.35

Note: Baseline cluster definition used. See text for definitions of the different education-specific job-creation and job-destruction measures. Industries with very few employees have been omitted for reasons of confidentiality.

Table A2. Surplus Job Creation 2002-2005, Baseline Cluster Definition and Alternative Cluster Definitions

	# Clusters	# ind	# reg	# edu	All firms SJC_A	GJC_A	NJC_A	Incumbent firms SJC_A^{in}	GJC_A^{in}	NJC_A^{in}	Start-up firms SJC_A^{su}	GJC_A^{su}	NJC_A^{su}	Start-ups' share of: GJC_A	SJC_A	Newness of jobs by: start-ups	incumbents
(1)	7,175	233	5	7	156,683	601,854	33,263	85,637	472,335	-96,256	71,046	129,519	129,519	0.22	0.45	0.55	0.18
(2)	35	1	5	7	55,134	601,854	33,263	14,895	472,335	-96,256	40,239	129,519	129,519	0.22	0.73	0.31	0.03
(3)	630	18	5	7	102,749	601,854	33,263	37,916	472,335	-96,256	64,833	129,519	129,519	0.22	0.63	0.50	0.08
(4)	2,585	77	5	7	130,013	601,854	33,263	61,021	472,335	-96,256	68,992	129,519	129,519	0.22	0.53	0.53	0.13
(5)	7,175	233	5	7	156,683	601,854	33,263	85,637	472,335	-96,256	71,046	129,519	129,519	0.22	0.45	0.55	0.18
(6)	17,532	617	5	7	200,725	601,854	33,263	128,236	472,335	-96,256	72,489	129,519	129,519	0.22	0.36	0.56	0.27
(7)	1,094	233	5	1	132,886	533,630	33,263	62,600	404,111	-96,256	70,286	129,519	129,519	0.24	0.53	0.54	0.15
(8)	7,175	233	5	7	156,683	601,854	33,263	85,637	472,335	-96,256	71,046	129,519	129,519	0.22	0.45	0.55	0.18
(9)	23,332	233	5	32	170,560	631,919	33,263	99,900	502,400	-96,256	70,660	129,519	129,519	0.20	0.41	0.55	0.20
(10)	1,597	233	1	7	128,912	601,854	33,263	59,715	472,335	-96,256	69,197	129,519	129,519	0.22	0.54	0.53	0.13
(11)	7,175	233	5	7	156,683	601,854	33,263	85,637	472,335	-96,256	71,046	129,519	129,519	0.22	0.45	0.55	0.18
(12)	13,781	233	12	7	180,836	601,854	33,263	107,538	472,335	-96,256	73,298	129,519	129,519	0.22	0.41	0.57	0.23
(13)	1	1	1	1	33,263	533,630	33,263	0	404,111	-96,256	33,263	129,519	129,519	0.24	1.00	0.26	0.00
(14)	80,221	617	12	32	254,573	631,919	33,263	179,010	502,400	-96,256	75,563	129,519	129,519	0.20	0.30	0.58	0.36

Note: Row 1 uses the baseline definition of a job cluster with seven education groups, five regions and 233 industries, while rows 2-14 use alternative job-cluster definitions. See text for definitions of the different education-specific job-creation and job-destruction measures.

TABLE A3. Job Creation by Education Groups, 2002-2007, Alternative Cluster Definition

	Employment in 2002	All firms			Incumbent firms			Start-up firms			Start-ups' share of:		Newness of jobs by:	
		GJC_A	NJC_A	SJC_A	GJC_A^{in}	NJC_A^{in}	SJC_A^{in}	GJC_A^{su}	NJC_A^{su}	SJC_A^{su}	GJC_A	SJC_A	start-ups	incumbents
Total	1,797,472	883,117	148,787	248,548	665,058	-69,272	108,301	218,059	218,059	140,247	0.25	0.56	0.64	0.16
By education group:														
Primary school	546,646	261,355	22,610	63,305	198,586	-40,159	23,191	62,769	62,769	40,114	0.24	0.63	0.64	0.12
Vocational education	718,244	291,302	16,971	58,278	213,246	-61,085	18,974	78,056	78,056	39,304	0.27	0.67	0.50	0.09
High school	169,680	97,504	18,042	24,369	74,400	-5,062	11,510	23,104	23,104	12,859	0.24	0.53	0.56	0.15
Short further education	83,793	47,704	16,218	18,336	37,529	6,043	10,006	10,175	10,175	8,330	0.21	0.45	0.82	0.27
Medium further education	130,209	74,486	27,488	31,023	56,046	9,048	15,017	18,440	18,440	16,006	0.25	0.52	0.87	0.27
Long further education	80,649	53,490	27,292	28,446	41,505	15,307	17,058	11,985	11,985	11,388	0.22	0.40	0.95	0.41
Unknown	68,251	57,276	20,166	24,791	43,746	6,636	12,545	13,530	13,530	12,246	0.24	0.49	0.91	0.29

Note: Cluster definition with 77 industries, 7 education groups and 5 regions used. See text for definitions of the different education-specific job-creation and job-destruction measures.

TABLE A4. Job Creation by Industry Groups, 2002-2007, Alternative Cluster Definition

	Employment in 2002	All firms			Incumbent firms			Start-up firms			Start-ups' share of:		Newness of jobs by:	
		GJC_A	NJC_A	SJC_A	GJC_A^{in}	NJC_A^{in}	SJC_A^{in}	GJC_A^{su}	NJC_A^{su}	SJC_A^{su}	GJC_A	SJC_A	start-ups	incumbents
Total	1,797,472	883,117	148,787	248,548	665,058	-69,272	108,301	218,059	218,059	140,247	0.25	0.56	0.64	0.16
By industry:														
Wholesale and retail trade	421,920	229,266	41,275	45,746	187,358	-633	17,480	41,908	41,908	28,266	0.18	0.62	0.67	0.09
Manufacturing	415,629	110,995	-24,496	21,214	95,458	-40,033	14,719	15,537	15,537	6,495	0.14	0.31	0.42	0.15
Construction	172,067	98,796	30,902	32,462	62,094	-5,800	4,358	36,702	36,702	28,104	0.37	0.87	0.77	0.07
Transportation	153,038	63,391	872	13,726	48,150	-14,369	6,829	15,241	15,241	6,897	0.24	0.50	0.45	0.14
Knowledge-based services	118,980	70,092	21,447	24,382	47,057	-1,588	7,299	23,035	23,035	17,083	0.33	0.70	0.74	0.16
Travel agent, cleaning and other operational services	109,030	85,775	44,108	47,287	65,679	24,012	31,529	20,096	20,096	15,758	0.23	0.33	0.78	0.48
Information and communication	95,426	56,648	2,704	12,897	44,396	-9,548	6,090	12,252	12,252	6,807	0.22	0.53	0.56	0.14
Accomodation and food service activities	89,428	65,471	16,166	16,589	39,884	-9,421	1,682	25,587	25,587	14,907	0.39	0.90	0.58	0.04
Financial and insurance	79,209	19,218	-659	8,028	17,154	-2,723	6,856	2,064	2,064	1,172	0.11	0.15	0.57	0.40
Education	30,009	13,509	4,334	4,773	12,189	3,014	3,930	1,320	1,320	843	0.10	0.18	0.64	0.32
Other service activities	29,145	14,980	-1,368	1,934	9,221	-7,127	177	5,759	5,759	1,757	0.38	0.91	0.31	0.02
Real estate activities	27,947	16,568	-572	2,736	10,732	-6,408	810	5,836	5,836	1,926	0.35	0.70	0.33	0.08
Arts, entertainment and other services	17,711	12,086	5,342	5,597	8,563	1,819	2,816	3,523	3,523	2,781	0.29	0.50	0.79	0.33
Human health and social work	17,443	14,368	6,945	7,028	7,881	458	1,514	6,487	6,487	5,514	0.45	0.78	0.85	0.19
Electricity, gas, steam and air conditioning supply	8,871	5,790	1,043	1,476	5,214	467	1,133	576	576	343	0.10	0.23	0.60	0.22
Water supply, sewerage and waste management	7,867	2,762	-481	694	2,480	-763	536	282	282	158	0.10	0.23	0.56	0.22
Mining and quarrying	2,294	664	-349	296	458	-555	174	206	206	122	0.31	0.41	0.59	0.38
Activity not stated	1,458	2,738	1,574	1,683	1,090	-74	369	1,648	1,648	1,314	0.60	0.78	0.80	0.34

Note: Cluster definition with 77 industries, 7 education groups and 5 regions used. See text for definitions of the different education-specific job creation and job-destruction measures.

TABLE A5. Job Creation by Education Groups without Regional Dimension, 2002-2007

	Employment in 2002	All firms			Incumbent firms			Start-up firms			Start-ups' share of:		Newness of jobs by:	
		GJC_A	NJC_A	SJC_A	GJC_A^{in}	NJC_A^{in}	SJC_A^{in}	GJC_A^{su}	NJC_A^{su}	SJC_A^{su}	GJC_A	SJC_A	start-ups	incumbents
Total	1,797,472	883,117	148,787	253,299	665,058	-69,272	117,037	218,059	218,059	136,262	0.25	0.54	0.62	0.18
By education group:														
Primary schooling	546,646	261,355	22,610	64,868	198,586	-40,159	28,413	62,769	62,769	36,455	0.24	0.56	0.58	0.14
Vocational education	718,244	291,302	16,971	58,918	213,246	-61,085	20,161	78,056	78,056	38,757	0.27	0.66	0.50	0.09
High school	169,680	97,504	18,042	27,160	74,400	-5,062	13,341	23,104	23,104	13,819	0.24	0.51	0.60	0.18
Short further education	83,793	47,704	16,218	18,624	37,529	6,043	10,431	10,175	10,175	8,193	0.21	0.44	0.81	0.28
Medium further education	130,209	74,486	27,488	30,936	56,046	9,048	14,580	18,440	18,440	16,356	0.25	0.53	0.89	0.26
Long further education	80,649	53,490	27,292	28,911	41,505	15,307	17,551	11,985	11,985	11,360	0.22	0.39	0.95	0.42
Unknown	68,251	57,276	20,166	23,882	43,746	6,636	12,560	13,530	13,530	11,322	0.24	0.47	0.84	0.29

Note: Cluster definition with 233 industries, seven education groups and one region used. See text for definitions of the different education-specific job-creation and job-destruction measures.

TABLE A6. Job Creation by Industry Groups without Regional Dimension, 2002-2007

	Employment in 2002	All firms			Incumbent firms			Start-up firms			Start-ups' share of:		Newness of jobs by:	
		GJC_A	NJC_A	SJC_A	GJC_A^{in}	NJC_A^{in}	SJC_A^{in}	GJC_A^{su}	NJC_A^{su}	SJC_A^{su}	GJC_A	SJC_A	start-ups	incumbents
Total	1,797,472	883,117	148,787	253,299	665,058	-69,272	117,037	218,059	218,059	136,262	0.25	0.54	0.62	0.18
By industry:														
Wholesale and retail trade	421,920	229,266	41,275	55,489	187,358	-633	28,369	41,908	41,908	27,120	0.18	0.49	0.65	0.15
Manufacturing	415,629	110,995	-24,496	19,272	95,458	-40,033	13,866	15,537	15,537	5,406	0.14	0.28	0.35	0.15
Construction	172,067	98,796	30,902	30,904	62,094	-5,800	3,662	36,702	36,702	27,242	0.37	0.88	0.74	0.06
Transportation	153,038	63,391	872	13,144	48,150	-14,369	7,040	15,241	15,241	6,104	0.24	0.46	0.40	0.15
Knowledge-based services	118,980	70,092	21,447	24,176	47,057	-1,588	5,982	23,035	23,035	18,194	0.33	0.75	0.79	0.13
Travel agent, cleaning and other operational services	109,030	85,775	44,108	46,954	65,679	24,012	32,933	20,096	20,096	14,021	0.23	0.30	0.70	0.50
Information and communication	95,426	56,648	2,704	12,079	44,396	-9,548	5,077	12,252	12,252	7,002	0.22	0.58	0.57	0.11
Accomodation and food service activities	89,428	65,471	16,166	16,610	39,884	-9,421	2,022	25,587	25,587	14,588	0.39	0.88	0.57	0.05
Financial and insurance	79,209	19,218	-659	8,307	17,154	-2,723	7,007	2,064	2,064	1,300	0.11	0.16	0.63	0.41
Education	30,009	13,509	4,334	4,442	12,189	3,014	3,672	1,320	1,320	770	0.10	0.17	0.58	0.30
Other service activities	29,145	14,980	-1,368	1,602	9,221	-7,127	83	5,759	5,759	1,519	0.38	0.95	0.26	0.01
Real estate activities	27,947	16,568	-572	3,439	10,732	-6,408	989	5,836	5,836	2,450	0.35	0.71	0.42	0.09
Arts, entertainment and other services	17,711	12,086	5,342	5,342	8,563	1,819	2,404	3,523	3,523	2,938	0.29	0.55	0.83	0.28
Human health and social work	17,443	14,368	6,945	7,418	7,881	458	1,932	6,487	6,487	5,486	0.45	0.74	0.85	0.25
Electricity, gas, steam and air conditioning supply	8,871	5,790	1,043	2,072	5,214	467	1,618	576	576	454	0.10	0.22	0.79	0.31
Water supply, sewerage and waste management	7,867	2,762	-481	370	2,480	-763	246	282	282	124	0.10	0.34	0.44	0.10
Mining and quarrying	2,294	664	-349	105	458	-555	37	206	206	68	0.31	0.65	0.33	0.08
Activity not stated	1,458	2,738	1,574	1,574	1,090	-74	98	1,648	1,648	1,476	0.60	0.94	0.90	0.09

Note: Cluster definition with 233 industries, seven education groups and one region used. See text for definitions of the different education-specific job-creation and job-destruction measures.